...BUT GOD...

The Forty Things That Happen To You The Instant You Become A Christian

BY: JIM SYLVESTER

...But God...
The Forty Things That Happen To You The Instant You Become
A Christian
by Jim Sylvester

Printed in the United States of America

ISBN 9781628717457

www.xulonpress.com

TABLE OF CONTENTS

———⌘———

POSITIONAL TRUTH SERIES
CHAPTER #1

———~∞~———

" *I* thought it was great when I received Christ that my sins were forgiven and that I was going to heaven. Now you're telling me *forty* things happened to me the moment I became a Christian?" That was the young man's earnest question. "Yes I am," came the reply, "and with the many challenges you as a believer and the church itself are facing, there is the need for all forty."

Relationship:

/ It was a major milestone anniversary for Mom and Dad. The children so desired to make it special. They pulled together enough funds to send their parents on a very splendid cruise. The night the family celebrated the anniversary they pulled out all the brochures. They showed their parents pictures of the beautiful ship, the layout of all the different decks on-board, maps of where they were sailing, and ports of call. Mom and Dad humbly and gratefully received the gift. Later that evening alone, they talked of their embarrassment. It had been a difficult economy. They didn't have the savings to afford to go on this nice trip the kids had purchased for them. But for the kids, they would make the best of it.

"Look Dear," the mom shared, "we can pack crackers and cheese and tea bags in our luggage. Maybe we can smuggle in some nuts and granola bars as well, and just enjoy the weather and beautiful sights."

So off they went. After a couple of days on one of those beautiful days at sea, they were up on deck and the aroma of a barbecue of baby back pork ribs and Texas Beef Brisket was wafting through the air. The dad's stomach rumbled and he couldn't take it any longer. He saw a ship's officer and approached him.

"Please, Sir, my wife and I were given a very wonderful gift of this cruise by our kids. We haven't been able to afford the cost of meals, so we have been surviving on the meager rations we brought aboard ship. Could we talk to you or the captain and work out a deal to maybe work on ship? We could clean, bus tables or do the laundry, anything to be able to eat some of the delicious food we see here."

"Oh, my," the officer replied. "That is so sad to hear. Weren't you aware of the conditions that go along with the purchase of a cruise? Actually, it is not only the food, but the movies, the shows, the dancing and games are all part of the package. It is *all* included. Your children purchased the whole package for you when they booked you on the cruise."

You know what is tragic? This is so often how we live the Christian life, on crackers and cheese. We become believers and just scrape by on our own provisions. After a while, in desperation we try to strike a deal with God. Maybe we can get a little more from God if we promise to do those extra chores.

Growth as a believer is not getting more from God. It is applying what is already true. With your position in Christ you are the most resourced individual on earth. You do not have to live in defeat; the victorious Christian life has been made possible for you. All you need to do is to learn what it means to be in Christ and what is yours as a result. Then, as you learn how to apply these truths in your life, they become real.

Forty things happened to you the instant you received Christ!

Eph. 1:3 "Blessed be the God and Father of our Lord Jesus Christ, who has blessed us with every spiritual blessing in the heavenly places in Christ,"

Notice, you have been blessed. It is a *completed* act. You have been blessed with *every* spiritual blessing. You lack nothing. Those spiritual blessings are from the heavenly places in Christ. And where are you? In Christ!

I came to Christ in high school through a Billy Graham crusade in my city. They gave me follow-up material that I faithfully filled out and mailed back. My spiritual high lasted for just a couple of months and then I started struggling with the same sins that led me to realize my need for Jesus as my Savior. My problem was that I did not know how to experience day-to-day victory. That was frustrating. I felt kind of hopeless. So after a while I put everything on the back burner and just existed as a very immature believer. Later I went away to college, while there I grabbed for everything college offered. My grades and grade point average didn't look too good after my first year, but then really improved until I was offered an assistantship to graduate school. I played a sport, was an officer in a fraternity, oversaw part of a men's dormitory as a resident hall advisor, and was involved in a top leadership position in student government.

You would think I would have felt fulfilled, but you know it all still left me empty with a lingering, hollow feeling. In my senior year, I fell in love and got engaged. It dawned on me that if I wanted to have a successful marriage like my parents had, I needed the Lord as a much more significant part of my life. The hard part was I had to swallow my pride. I took my fiancé to the church my folks were attending at the time, and we walked in and sat right next to them. I hadn't been to church for three years. This was an act of surrender for me. My mom was so shocked she just about passed out. I later found out my dad reached over and touched her knee and said, "Act normal!" Fortunately for me she did.

Through that church and getting involved with a Christian student movement in graduate school I began to see God work wonderfully in my life as well as on my campus. As a very young believer I saw God answer prayers on an hourly basis! My wife Jan and I got involved with the student movement and God's word opened up to us. We experienced complete forgiveness. We learned how to see victory over sin. We enjoyed the experience of a personal relationship with Jesus. We also were learning how to step out in faith. Our student movement grew from fifty to one hundred to one hundred and fifty in just months. We believed God for our campus and the world and saw Him work powerfully in so many lives in so many ways. We were learning to live for that which is eternal, not temporal.

In the spring of that year I went to a weekend retreat with Josh McDowell. He was teaching from the book of Romans sharing his series called, "The Revolutionary Revelation". In this series Josh explained positional truth and what it meant to be in Christ. He so motivated me through this series. Two weeks later I drove a few hours to another campus to hear Josh share the same series again. I longed to understand all that was true of me as a believer and I set out to study the Word diligently. One of the first things I did was to color code my Bible. I would underline every verse in green that related to salvation, in purple every verse that related to the Deity of Christ, in orange every verse related to being "in Christ" or all that was true about us "with Christ". I started with twelve different colors and other doctrines including the attributes of God, the ministry of the Holy Spirit, messianic prophecy and second coming prophecy. With regard to positional truth forty things stood out to me. I hope to share all forty of these with you through this series. They fell into these six categories:

1) Intimacy in your **Relationship** with God.
2) Your **Rest and Righteousness** in Christ.
3) The **Restrainer** and your experience of the ministry of the Holy Spirit.
4) The **Resources** you need for the everyday battles involved in fulfilling the Great Commission.
5) Your **Rights** for the Spiritual Battle with the forces of darkness.
6) Your destiny as **Royalty** and your throne room privileges

When people receive Jesus Christ into their lives, the most powerful awesome living Christ comes to dwell within them. When a person receives Christ, he or she receives all that there is to receive. One needs nothing more. If you lack power or victory or the abundance that God has promised, it is not because you lack an experience or you need to get something from God. *You have all you need!* You have Christ! What you need to do is to apply in your life those things God has already made true about you. So let's get started.

1) <u>You are Alive</u>

> John 3:3-5 "Jesus answered and said to him, "Truly, truly, I say to you, unless one is born again he cannot see the kingdom of God." Nicodemus said to Him, "How can a man be born when he is old? He cannot enter a second time into his mother's womb and be born, can he?" Jesus answered, "Truly, truly, I say to you, unless one is born of water and the Spirit he cannot enter into the kingdom of God. That which is born of the flesh is flesh, and that which is born of the Spirit is spirit."

Nicodemus meets Jesus at night. This is a safer, a more private time for him as a leader of Israel to ask Jesus a question. The Lord sees right into Nic's heart and responds, "One must be born again." Nic sees a dilemma. A grown man cannot enter his mother's womb again. This is not physically possible, nor would she be receptive to the idea. Jesus informs him that there are two births. The first birth is physical. When a woman's water breaks she is set to deliver her child. That which is born of the flesh is flesh. There is a second birth which is spiritual and enables one to enter the kingdom of God. That which is born of the Spirit is spirit. Spiritual birth is necessary because we see in Eph. 2:1-3 the condition of one who is only born once.

> "And you were dead in your trespasses and sins, in which you formerly walked according to the course of this world, according to the prince of the power of the air, of the spirit that is now working in the sons of disobedience. Among them we too all formerly lived in the lusts of our flesh, indulging the desires of the flesh and of the mind, and were by nature children of wrath, even as the rest."

What is a person's relationship like with God who is in this condition?
- They are d*ead,*
- *Walking according to the course of the world,*
- *according to the prince of the power of the air,*
- *a son of disobedience,*

- *living in the lusts of the flesh,*
- *a child of wrath.*

Not a very pretty picture.

Have you ever unexpectedly come upon a dead animal?

Think of your response. It was probably shocking and rather unpleasant.

I was visiting the University of Southern California and was on campus meeting with the team leader of the ministry. We were visiting a student in one of the dorms who told us a story that had just occurred in his dorm less than a week earlier. It seems a couple of young men who lived in the dorm had gone fishing and had caught a very, very large cod fish. They thought it would be quite the prank to hide it in the men's community bathroom above the ceiling tiles. Within no time the odor in the bathroom became extremely unpleasant. Men would come in and shout, "Who got sick in here?" It was only a matter of hours and the smell in there was so foul that guys were going to different floors to use a restroom. By the next day men couldn't stand to be on the floor. Pretty soon the whole dorm reeked. When the dorm maintenance went in to check on the source of the horrendous odor even holding their nose they almost threw up. As they looked at the ceiling there was a huge wet brown spot with a thick ugly dripping liquid falling onto the floor. It was rank. By now university officials had been informed and they sent a professional cleaning crew in, but it was so bad, that even with masks they couldn't stand it. Ultimately they sent a team that looked so ridiculous you would almost think they were toxic waste specialists. They weren't. Wearing hazmat suits they removed the dead, dripping, diseased, disgusting fish from the ceiling and sprayed the place down with disinfectant.

My Dear Friend, that cod fish was you! You and I were spiritually just that dead, that offensive and that repulsive. We were so diseased by sin, that we looked like that grotesque dripping animal under God's wrath. Isn't that what Paul is telling us here in Ephesians? As repulsive as a dead decaying creature would be to us, dead sinners are many times more offensive to the Lord. Truly He is wondrously holy and sinless. God, because of His nature, is utterly offended by

10

sin. Yet He loves humanity, so Paul continues here in Ephesians 2:4 with these two great words, "But God".

> Eph.2:4-6 " But God, being rich in mercy, because of His great love with which He loved us, even when we were dead in our transgressions, made us alive together with Christ (by grace you have been saved), and raised us up with Him, and seated us with Him in the heavenly places in Christ Jesus,

Now Reader, could you imagine going up to that dead animal, bending down, picking up that gross fish, pressing it to your chest and giving that slimy creature an embrace? Would you take it home and make it part of your family?

Think about it. Isn't that what God did and more? He took us as filthy, dead, diseased ones in sin, as creatures who were allied with the enemy of God and our own souls. We were so offensive that we had the sentence of eternal death upon us. We were under God's wrath! Now Paul uses this wonderful transition, "But GOD!!" When God intervenes in our lives He changes everything. He made us alive and He placed us "in Christ". God has reached you, believer. He took you as repulsive as one who is in sin would be to Him. He breathed the breath of spiritual life into you and made you His very own. He wrapped His arms around you and took you home with Him.

We are spiritually alive! We are able to have a relationship with Him who is life itself. We can know God, hear His voice, speak His language, think and understand His thoughts. The Bible, His Word, makes sense to us. How radically does this change you?

We take with us the fragrance of life. We take that with us everywhere we go as opposed to the stench of death. We are a breath of freshness, with the very Life of God in us.

He made the lifeless alive!

God has given us His life, Spiritual life.

This is who you are, a life living and a life giving person. God's spiritual life pulses through and in you. As you think rightly about yourself you are able to act in character as who you truly are. You are alive to God.

2) <u>An Intimate Personal Family Relationship</u>

Deeply ingrained in my heart is the memory of the day our son Dan came into our lives. We were at the office of the attorney who helped us with the adoption. He walked in holding this precious boy, my son, Dan. I looked at Jan, looked at the attorney and reached out my arms. Oh, the joy of being able to hold my son for the first time. You may have children and can relate to how you are instantly in love. Or if you don't have children, imagine how your heart will feel. I thought, "Lord, could You possibly feel about me as I feel about my son?" I heard the Lord say in that quiet voice, "I love you like that my son, and more." You, beloved, have an intimate personal family relationship. God is your Father.

John 1:12,13 "But as many as received Him, to them He gave the right to become children of God, even to those who believe in His name, who were born, not of blood nor of the will of the flesh nor of the will of man, but of God."

What does it mean to you to be a child of God and to know him as Father? What happens in your heart when you contemplate the idea of a father?

Our relationship with our human fathers in so many ways shapes our view of God. You may have had a very good relationship with your dad. You may have been very close to him and you were able to share your hearts with one another. He was always available to you. He had time for you. You longed to see him and he was there when you needed him and he would do all he could to come through for you.

If so, it is not hard for you to believe that your heavenly Father loves you deeply and that He longs to spend time with you. He wants to hear your heart. He wants to be needed by you. He so wants you to grow to your fullest potential and He delights in your every step and stumble along the way.

If your relationship with your human father was difficult, I imagine your view of God has been hindered. Do you act as if the Lord is someone you cannot please? .... Do you feel that you never seem to do enough to be accepted? .... Are you afraid to be real with Him? .... Does He seem distant and impersonal? .... Are you afraid

He will let you down? .... Do you believe you are too small and insignificant for Him to bother with? These are lies from the pit; God your father has none of these characteristics. He is your loving caring father and this needs to be real for you. Imagine yourself alone with Him in a very secure place. Lean in close to Him and allow Him to speak this truth into your heart. "I love you my child, you are mine." Embrace Him as Abba.

God the Father is the perfect father. Jesus is so intent on our understanding this that He brings it to light repeatedly in His teaching recorded in John's gospel. Jesus shares about His relationship with the Father and the intimacy He enjoys with Him. The Father is the source of what Jesus does, the example which Jesus models and the love Jesus experiences. Each aspect of His relationship is described to us so that we might understand our role as God's children.

I am imperfect, so flawed, yet how my daughter feels about me is overwhelming. One day when she was about six years old she was walking barefoot outside and stepped on a thorn which imbedded itself deep into her heel. Having heard of the problem and under-standing the pain she was in I hurried home. As I walked in I could see that numerous people were trying to care for her and they could not get her to hold still. The thorn was deep and I could tell it really hurt and even more so as someone tried to dig it out. They were being so sweet with her but she was scared. Seeing me she said, "I want Daddy to do it!" Talk about having your heart melt. She amazed me. As I took her foot into my hands you could feel her whole body relax. She was totally trusting and allowed me to dig with a needle under the thorn and extract it, I am sure with no less pain and possibly more than she was experiencing with others. There was calmness, a trust that the one who loved her would only hurt her as much as was necessary to remove the thorn. With her father she was safe.

Beloved, your heavenly Father wants you to deeply believe that He is ABBA. With Him you are safe and secure. No one loves you more. You have a place where you belong, in His family as His beloved child. You are extremely valuable to Him. He knows the number of hairs on your head. Jesus tells us how he cares for the sparrows and that we are infinitely more valuable than they. You are worth so much to Him that the precious Son of the Father died for you. We grow through His care and instruction into whole mature people. Sometimes when He has to remove a thorn from our lives, there is pain, but in the gracious hands of the Father we can trust ABBA will be as tender as possible through the whole process. To this day my daughter Chelle amazes me. We will sit to watch a movie and she'll lay her head on me and in no time, in a place she feels utterly safe, she falls asleep.

How about you with the Heavenly Father? Is there some growing that you need in your view of who He is? .... How do you see Him? .... Is He your protection? .... Do you feel safest with Him? .... Is He your source of strength and provision? .... Does His being Father draw you to Him? .... Being His child leads to intimacy because you are alive and you are His precious child. You are a son or daughter of the God of the universe. Enjoy being His child! If you haven't done this yet I encourage you again to imagine the Lord walking up to you and wrapping His arms around you and giving you the biggest, warmest bear hug. Share your heart with Him.

3) <u>Christ in You</u>

2 Cor. 13:5 "Test yourselves to see if you are in the faith; examine yourselves! Or do you not recognize this about yourselves that Jesus Christ is in you-unless indeed you fail the test?"

Col.1:27 "to whom God willed to make known what is the riches of the glory of this mystery among the Gentiles, which is Christ in you, the hope of glory."

Talk about the possibility of a close relationship. He lives in you! We, as believers, are all indwelt by the Lord. We carry His presence. If we had that mindset it would change how we approach our opportunities. It would change how we carry ourselves.

Think of Who it is Who indwells you. He is Creator, the King of the universe! That's quite the potential you have there!

Phil. 4:13 "I can do *all things* through Christ who strengthens me."

When you walk into a room, Who arrives along with you? Creator, God the Son, that's who. See how that will change your thoughts about yourself. How do you see yourself?

You are not only a representative of the Lord, you literally carry Him with you. Life is very hard yet we are able to minister in His presence and through His strength even when we face overwhelming trials.

The Lord has used this understanding in many ways for Jan and me. Let me share with you some of the struggles she and I have faced. Our first struggle was infertility. We were poked, prodded and put through many procedures. The Lord used this. We wrestled hard with Him, but came to understand that *He* is enough. We fell in love with our students as our disciples. We had the time and attention to give them not having our own children. The Lord gave grace and rich relationships and changed lives.

Years later we were able to adopt a little girl who we soon discovered had a congenital heart defect. There was the constant fear of losing her. We had night after night of close calls. She was never able to sleep for more than two hours at a time. That was because she could only consume two ounces of formula before she became exhausted from the strain of feeding and would pass out. Two hours later she would wake up from hunger and we would go through the whole process again. The Lord used this experience to build sensitivity and empathy into our hearts. He gave us the strength to handle night after night of the fatigue we experienced as Jan and I took turns being up all night with our little one. She had heart surgery just before her first birthday and within a few years we discovered that she was going to have a lifetime of special needs. There was real sadness realizing our precious daughter would be very limited by her disability. We mourned the loss of our daughter's ability to pick up on other people's personal communication, including ours. It is a deep loss for us that she is unable to share her own heart's depth with us. Now the growth in our lives was teaching us how to love, period, not receiving anything in return. To be honest it also built into us a deep longing for heaven where our little girl will be whole.

Later on, Jan, my beloved, was struck with cancer. That was a wholly frightening time. When a loved one has cancer you feel so helpless. All I could do was love her and let her know that no matter what she was always going to be my beautiful bride. The Lord who indwells us gave us His wonderful presence and His much needed strength to trust Him and walk with Him through it all. For Jan, this was a time of complete surrender to the Lord, trusting Him to do with her as He deemed best. She had wonderful doctors and the Lord brought her through and we are so grateful she is now completely cancer free.

I am now the one facing health issues. I have diabetes and I also have rheumatoid arthritis. I have to deal every day with the limits that these conditions create. So many times I feel the loss as I remember what I used to be physically. My son is a great athlete and is capable in many sports, and I get sad and frustrated that I cannot get out on the field and mix it up with him. Fortunately I had hand surgery recently so we can now toss a football around. There are losses yet the Lord has to give me the discipline and the ability to handle the restrictions, the pain and the fatigue. And what is amazing is that He supplies the strength for one step and the next step and then the one following that. Each day is an opportunity to step out in faith and watch the Lord supply as He chooses.

Like Paul, you and I can say, "I can do all things through Christ who strengthens me." Brothers and sisters, you are indwelt by the living Christ. He is intimately with you. His strength enables you and me to face whatever He allows to come our way. You carry God the Son with you into every experience. That ought to affect your expectations of being used of Him. Also consider this. It also ought to affect your choices. Do you wish to carry Him into sin? You see since we carry Him everywhere the sobering reality is "Would Jesus wish to do what I'm doing, go where I'm going or watch what I'm watching?" Christ is in you. Wow, what a privilege!

4) Eternal Life with a Resurrected Body- You Are Eternal

"For this is the will of My Father, that everyone who beholds the Son and believes in Him will have eternal life, and I Myself will raise him up on the last day." John 6:40

16

You and I were created for the eternal. So many times our feelings about life hint at this. There is the purchase that ends up being such a short lived pleasure. There is the experience so long looked forward to that does not deliver. We are let down time and again by imperfection. It should be better. Weren't we intended for more? There is something missing. Life contains sadness, pain, hurt and tragedy. Is this all there is? Eccl. 1:2 "Vanity of vanities," says the Preacher, "Vanity of vanities! All is vanity." Yet innately we sense this is not all there is and the things we fill our lives with that are not eternal do not satisfy our souls.

> Eccl. 3:11 "He has made everything beautiful in its time. He has also set eternity in the hearts of men; yet they cannot fathom what God has done from beginning to end" (NIV)

> 2 Cor. 4:18 "So we fix our eyes not on what is seen, but on what is unseen. For what is seen is temporary, but what is unseen is eternal."

1. When we die what happens?

> 2 Cor. 5:1,2,8 "Now we know that if the earthly tent we live in is destroyed, we have a building from God, an eternal house in heaven, not built by human hands. Meanwhile we groan, longing to be clothed with our heavenly dwelling." ... We are confident, I say, and would prefer to be away from the body and at home with the Lord."

Death in the Scriptures refers to separation. When one dies physically, the real self is separated from the body. When one is dead spiritually it means that our real self is separated from God. To die eternally means that the real self is forever separated from God in a place created for the devil and his demons. So when a believer dies physically, his or her body is laid in the grave but the real self goes into the presence of the Lord in heaven.

2. As the last days of history unfold, what happens?

> 2 Cor. 4:14 "knowing that He who raised the Lord Jesus
> will raise us also with Jesus and bring us with you into His
> presence." (ESV)

> Phil 3:21 "Who, by the power that enables Him to bring
> everything under His control, will transform our lowly bodies
> so that they will be like His glorious body." (NIV)

Jesus will call first the dead in Christ and then those who are
still alive to meet Him in the air. He will change that which is
mortal into an immortal body like His own resurrected body. This
is something wonderfully unique and special about God's purposes
as revealed in the New Testament. It differs greatly from Greek
philosophy where the body is treated as something bad. That is not
so in Christianity where the body is God's gift, something that He
Himself took in the incarnation. We will have a glorified resurrected
body throughout eternity.

3. What will eternal life be like?

> "Now this is eternal life: that they may know You, the only
> true God, and Jesus Christ, whom You have sent." John 17:3

We will be in a dear and intimate relationship with the Lord. It is a
relationship that will exist through all eternity, an eternity of growing
in our understanding of all the precious things about Him. The extent
and depth of His person will take all of forever to enjoy and explore.
It will be an existence where we as believers will be without sin.
Think of it, never having a bad thought or action; never uttering an
inappropriate or hurtful word. We will have perfect bodies that are
capable of expressing all our talents and abilities and all that without
pain or old age. We will be there together enjoying great fellowship
with one another, celebrating with believers from all the ages past.
For me it will be special as I will see my little girl in her true and full
potential. My heart longs to say, "There you are, Chelle!"

Life does not have to work out perfectly here. "Why?" you ask? Because this is not our only shot! You are eternal! You will have an eternity, one that is yet future and with an existence in a perfect environment with a perfect body enjoying the absolutely perfect God. Here is the kicker. Though you do not have the resurrected body at present, you have begun eternal life. Jesus said, "This is eternal life that we may know You the only true God and Jesus Christ whom You have sent." As a believer you have already begun to live eternally in a relationship with God.

"When we've been there 10,000 years bright shining as the sun we have no less days to sing His praise than when we first begun." (4th verse "Amazing Grace")

You are Eternal!

5) <u>**You Are Light**</u>

Eph.5:8-11 "For at one time you were darkness, but now you are light in the Lord. Walk as children of light (for the fruit of light is found in all that is good and right and true), and try to discern what is pleasing to the Lord. Take no part in the unfruitful works of darkness, but instead expose them." (ESV)

There are two kingdoms. The Lord's kingdom is the kingdom of light and the satanic kingdom is the kingdom of darkness. When we walk in the light, we walk in fellowship with the Lord and with other believers.

1 John 1:5-7 "God is light; in Him there is no darkness at all. If we claim to have fellowship with Him yet walk in the darkness, we lie and do not live by the truth. But if we walk in the light, as He is in the light, we have fellowship with one another, and the blood of Jesus, his Son, purifies us from all sin." (NIV)

You have likely noticed that when people discover that you are a Christian they put you under scrutiny. There is now a high standard

19

that they place you under. It is not fair of course, but that's what people do.

I have a friend who told me her story of working at a restaurant. When people found out she was a believer they started to treat her strangely. It was like they were watching her every move. Conversations would change when she would walk up to people. They would say to her, "You make me feel funny. I change my language around you. I can't be normal."

On one of those days when everything was sped up and customers filled the place, she was coming toward a swinging door with a tray full of food and she did not notice that it was swinging out, so she approached as it swung back and her whole tray and all its contents smashed to the tile floor, loudly enough that the whole restaurant and kitchen stopped and stared. Well, she lost it, she screamed and swore and kicked dishes around in anger.

Finally she knelt down to pick up the mess. As she did that one of her co-workers walked by and said, "Ha, and you call yourself a Christian." Some minutes went by. She finished picking it all up and mopped the floor. Later she was able to find the co-worker and humbly said, "You know you were right. I messed up. I guess this is just one of the reasons I need a Savior."

What is true about light? Light makes things visible. It exposes. Light is beautiful and reveals other things of beauty. Light brings freshness to our lives. When we are in a strong position spiritually the Lord enlightens our minds. Later when we get out of that atmosphere we might begin to question decisions we made at that time of spiritual strength. A very important principle I would tell students I worked with on summer leadership projects is, "Don't doubt later in the darkness what you have decided while walking in the light."

What is true about darkness? If all you know is darkness, you don't really know that you are in darkness. Until you come into the light, or have some contact with light you have no idea what you are missing. There may be a vague emptiness, but all you have to compare anything to is darkness. As Pastor Tony Evans would say, "Walk into darkness with a light and you immediately become the focus, and you are the one who can show the way."

Another way to think of light is how it brings hope and freshness to life. When a friend or loved one has a stay in the hospital we desire to send flowers. The desire is to cheer them, to express love, to brighten the environment in their room. We send flowers to a funeral or to be placed at a grave. These are to be a comfort and a fragrant display of life and hope in these palaces of loss.

Paul writes in Eph. 5:8,9 " for you were formerly darkness, but now you are Light in the Lord ; walk as children of Light for the fruit of the Light consists in all goodness and righteousness and truth."

You and I have been sent to this world that is filled with darkness to be a bouquet of flowers, a fragrance of His light and love. Have you realized that you can be the best thing to happen to a person today? What are you like when you are standing in a long line at the store? How about going through all the hassle of airport security? Are we as believers a fragrant aroma to the people who have to put up with people's complaints all day? Are we the most positive experience of their day?

You and I are light and as light makes things stand out, you and I ought to be outstanding.

You and I are light and as light we are so refreshing we can bring freshness to a stale world.

You are the Light of the World. (Mt.5:14)

Believer, you are alive, you are a son or daughter, Christ is in you and you are eternal.

6) <u>The hope of a personal home prepared by Jesus</u>

Home! Everyone needs a place where they belong, a place to call their own. Everyone needs a home. Life is very hard, but the thought of home brings hope and strength to make it through. When I am in the hospital I just want to go home. After a long trip overseas it is good to come home and sleep in my own bed. Home is such a special place.

Our literature is filled with many references to home. It touches us deeply in the stories of a soldier who hears from home, E.T. who wants to phone home, a father who makes it home for Christmas, an orphan who is chosen to come home with a childless couple. In the movie Gladiator where Maximus sees the ashes of his family and home destroyed, but in the final scene has a vision of eternity going home to his wife and daughter.

Dear friends, Jesus tells us that heaven is home because we will live there with Him forever. He needed to say this because in John chapter 13 He had just said to His disciples, "I am going away and where I am going you cannot come now."

This totally frustrated Peter who wanted to know, "Lord where are you going and why can't I follow You, right now?" Peter also promised, "I will lay down my life for you." That did not go too well for Peter. Jesus informed him that he would actually deny Him before dawn. Following this, Jesus says to all the disciples, "Let not your heart be troubled." He goes on to tell us He is making a home for each and every one of us. That home will be wonderful because He personally is the one preparing it.

John 14:1-3 "Do not let your heart be troubled; believe in God, believe also in Me. In My Father's house are many dwelling places; if it were not so, I would have told you; for I go to prepare a place for you. If I go and prepare a place for you, I will come again and receive you to Myself, that where I am, there you may be also."

I was on a staff team with a very dear woman, Lisa Nieman. Lisa is an outstanding speaker and I may never have heard a better illustration than one she personally used to illustrate heaven in a message she shared.

Lisa was about eight months pregnant. She walked to the front of the auditorium in front of a few hundred students and set on the table beside her a bassinette. She was so endearing. She appeared very adorable in her lovely maternity outfit. She had the students thinking home and mom before she began. She proceeded to share some very profound insights about the Lord's many attributes. We know a great deal about Him as God the Father. She went on to explain that rarely are His matriarchal attributes recognized. For example, God gives birth and God is a homemaker, she said, using this passage here in John fourteen to support her points. Then she said, "This bassinette I have before you I have spent hours of creative energy to make. I want it to be so beautiful. What do you think? Did I do alright?" she asked. Of course she was reinforced resoundingly. "I want it to be warm and comfortable," she went on. "I want this to be home for my child and I have poured my heart into it." Next she shared, "You know I do not know much about this child. I don't even know if the child will be a boy or a girl so I don't even know its name. And here is something else to consider. My child will not use this as home for much more than six months." Then she applied her point. Jesus is making a home for you and He knows you intimately. He is making for you a personal, eternal home.

Let me pick up from there. Dear One, Jesus knows your heart, your longings, and your dreams. When you get home to heaven you will walk into the place Jesus has made just for you. You will be so touched that He knows your favorite colors. You will turn the corner and it will catch your breath that He captured your deepest longings, and that He anticipated your every dream. He is making this place for you that will celebrate your richest moments with Him and your most wonderful memories and greatest accomplishments. It will have things He made just for you. You will never feel more at home than with Him there in the place ideally suited for you. Oh yeah, you will only have all of eternity to enjoy it! There is so much that He will have put into it that all of eternity is what you will need. What an incredible hope. Believer you have begun that relationship with Him now. Make the most of that every day.

You have a home in heaven that bathes every aspect of your life in absolute significance. There is such a search for significance in every society on our planet. There is a longing within each individual for a meaningful identity. Here is yours, Believer. The living God, wanting to have a personal relationship with you, made true about you the instant you became a Christian:

1. You are spiritually alive.
2. You have a heavenly Father and are a precious child of God.
3. The most powerful infinite Christ dwells within you.

4. You are an eternal being who will have a resurrected body.
5. You are light.
6. You have a wonderful hope of a personal home pre-pared by Jesus.

All this is to enhance and make possible a personal relationship with God.

Life versus Death
His Child vs. His Enemy
Indwelt vs. Separated
Eternal vs. Temporal
Light vs. Darkness
A Home built with perfect specifications vs. being Homeless

The story goes that there was a couple who were on their way home after fifty years on the mission field. They had given their lives for the sake of the gospel to a people who had been an unreached people group. They were on a train only minutes away from their final destination. As they got closer their anticipation grew. They began to wonder. We have kept folks informed of our progress. Do you think anyone will care we are back? Will there be any one at the station to welcome us back?

They gathered their belongings as the train rounded a bend and they could see the platform. Oh, that platform was filled with people and, their hearts jumped. They moved to the door and got in line. Before they disembarked a band struck up, the people cheered and a local political leader stepped out to be welcomed by the crowd. They all moved off following behind the leader. The couple stepped out onto an empty platform. No one was there to meet them. He looked at his wife and from a deeply choked up throat said, "Fifty years, fifty years we served the Savior and did no one care? We gave our hearts and the strength of our years and now we return, and there is no one here to welcome us home." The wife got face to face with him, looked him straight in the eye and lovingly said, "Remember, my love, we have not arrived at our true home yet!"

POSITIONAL TRUTH SERIES
CHAPTER #2

Standing in His <u>Righteousness:</u>

The second aspect of positional truth that we will tackle relates to our standing in Christ. It is a standing in His righteousness. It is my hope that these Biblical truths will affect your understanding of your total acceptance in the Lord. You are at peace with God if you have trusted Christ as your personal Savior. You have the Lord's approval completely. It is also my hope that you will be gripped by these truths, and as you are, it will lead to your sense of security, impact how you step out in faith and how you confidently approach the Lord.

As Jan and I began our career we were able to take some classes with some of the finest seminary professors in the United States. One of the classes was a course on Soteriology (Salvation) taught by a professor who we were warned was one of the most academically challenging we would ever study under. Past students teased that he shared so much Biblical material that if you simply dropped your pen you would be a whole page behind in your notes. The time for the midterm came. The professor passed out the exams. It was a little comical to hear the sounds coming from the students. There were deep sighs, as well as exclamations like "What?" "No way!" and "Is he serious?" Our professor's response was, "Quiet, please, Men and Women. You have a lot of work before you".

We were asked to share all the parallels between Leviticus and the book of Hebrews, sighting all the verses by memory without consulting a Bible. We were required to list and describe every "type" (historical person or example) in the Old Testament that pictured salvation in Christ, again quoting verses by memory. We needed to list all the words that related to salvation like redemption, propitiation, atonement and reconciliation, defining all twelve words on the list and quoting from memory verses that support and contain these words and or concepts. We had to show where election was taught in the Word from no less than four passages, again quoting all verses from memory. We were asked to share our personal position on this subject and defend that position Biblically. There was more but I think you get the idea. At the end of two hours not one of us had completed the exam, but we turned them in and headed out.

We gathered out in the hall and slowly began to reveal to one another how we felt about how we had done. The first one of us sheepishly said, "I don't think I did too well." "Really, me either," someone piped in. The ice was broken so someone shared, "You know, I think I flunked it." "Me too," someone gladly added. Then one of us with a broad smile shared, "I was so far below "C" level I drowned." We started giving each other high fives. We were pumped up. We were sure that the burden was on the professor. Surely, he couldn't flunk the whole class!

The next Monday in class he passed back the tests. We started straining our necks to see the grades marked on each of our tests. They were all marked with big red circled "F's" (for failure). We subtly gave each other thumbs up.

The professor stood at the front of the class and said, "Men and Women, I am so surprised and disappointed. You all flunked the exam."

Still certain that we had some security in our mutual failure, we asked, "What are you going to do? Will you give us a new test? Will you grade on a curve? Will you throw it out or let us take it home, correct it and return it to you?"

"No! Most definitely I will not!" He answered. He continued, "Are you not all in leadership with this movement? And what is your job? Isn't it to share the gospel?"

"Yes," we meekly replied.

"You know, Men and Women, people's eternal destinies are involved here and this is a course on salvation and you want me to pass you and ignore that you failed?"

It sunk in that we were in trouble. "By the way", the professor continued, "there is someone who passed this test."

Who? We thought, and began to look around to see who it was that had ruined it for all of us. Who was it that stabbed us in the back? The looks on our faces were scary.

"There is one person who got a one hundred percent, the professor stated, and it was none of you so you can save your disdain. It was me."

We sarcastically intoned, "You! Of course! You're the professor. You made up the test, and you are the author of the course textbook!"

"True!" he agreed and then added, "Yet I do have something to offer you. Here is my grade book and, as you can see, there is an "F" beside each of your names. I am willing to replace your "F" with my "one hundred percent" if you will make a simple acknowledgement of this by individually saying to me, 'Professor, I failed the test. My grade totally missed the needed requirement. I gratefully accept the free gift of your grade as my own.' "

So the professor approached the first student, who, visibly struggling, responded, "Seriously Sir? I can have your one hundred percent? So, what's the catch? Isn't there a way I can take this over? I know I could do better. I bet I did better than most of the other students!"

Yes, I'm joking. Although there were possibly thoughts like that in the classroom that day, no one responded that way. We understood his point and took the illustration as clear instruction about justification by faith, and we gladly rejoiced, taking his one hundred percent as our own. Do you connect with this, Believer? That you received as a free gift the one hundred percent divine righteousness of Christ? It was imputed to you. You were declared righteous, as righteous as the Lord Himself.

Let's learn about your imputed righteousness through the next five truths that happened to you the instant you became a Christian.

7) <u>All My Sin Totally Paid For</u>

Heb. 10:1-9 "For the Law, since it has only a shadow of the good things to come and not the very form of things, can never, by the same sacrifices which they offer continually year by year, make perfect those who draw near. Otherwise, would they not have ceased to be offered, because the worshipers, having once been cleansed, would no longer have had consciousness of sins? But in those sacrifices there is a reminder of sins year by year. For it is impossible for the blood of bulls and goats to take away sins. Therefore, when He comes into the world, He says, "SACRIFICE AND OFFERING YOU HAVE NOT DESIRED, BUT A BODY YOU HAVE PREPARED FOR IN WHOLE BURNT OFFERINGS AND SACRAFICES FOR SIN YOU HAVE TAKEN NO PLEASURE."THEN I SAID, 'BEHOLD, I HAVE COME IN THE SCROLL OF THE BOOK IT IS WRITTEN TO DO YOUR WILL, O GOD.' "After saying above, "SACRIFICES AND OFFERINGS AND WHOLE BURNT OFFERINGS AND sacrifices FOR SIN YOU HAVE NOT DESIRED, NOR HAVE YOU TAKEN PLEASURE in them" (which are offered according to the Law), then He said, "BEHOLD, I HAVE COME TO DO YOUR WILL." He takes away the first in order to establish the second. "

The Old Testament sacrificial system is very much in the writer's mind as he talks about what has happened to our sin. The Law of Moses had a moral requirement for the people. They were required to keep each and every one of the Lord's commandments. For examples: "You are to be holy as I am holy". They learned of His Holiness as they learned of and endeavored to keep His commands.

There was also a picture of the Lord's purity and holiness through the cleansing requirements of the law. These were requirements that pictured the Lord's purity and how His people were not to defile themselves. The priests who served in the sanctuary were to perform cleansing and purification before even entering the first part of the tabernacle. All this to picture how high and holy the Lord God of Israel is.

The Israelites learned of the distance between their holy God and themselves as they understood the way they approached the Lord through the sacrificial system. The design of the Tabernacle and then the Temple spoke of distance. Only a priest from the tribes of Levi of the family of Aaron could go into the holy place and offer a sacrifice. All other Israelites were excluded. This was particularly illustrated on Yom Kippur, the Day of Atonement. The High Priest was the only one who could enter through the curtain that separated the holy place from the Holy of Holies, and he could do that just once a year on the Day of Atonement. The High Priest would wash himself in prescribed ways. Then he would make sacrifices for his own sins before he could represent the people. He laid his hands upon the sacrificial animal symbolically transferring his and all of the people's sins upon the animal.

The one goat would be slain and its blood poured out. A second goat known as the "Scape Goat" would be released into the wilderness symbolically carrying away with him the people's sins, never to be found. The High Priest would then enter the Holy of Holies. While in there he would take the blood and sprinkle it upon the mercy seat, picturing the blood as a covering for sin. These actions of the High Priest demonstrate the Lord's holiness and the people's distance from that purity.

Here is another issue raised about these sacrifices: they were offered over and over and over again. The sins of the future remained to be covered the next time and the next. Each and every sacrifice was only a reminder of sins merely being covered, not completely taken away. So they repeated these sacrifices time after time after time.

I have the disease known as diabetes. I take pills with every meal and a shot of insulin every night. Every time I do these things I am not cured, I am just reminded that I have this disease. I will do this over and over again for the rest of my life. This was true of the Old Testament believer who faithfully offered these sacrifices over and over again. It never made him perfect. It just reminded him, "I am a sinner." These sacrifices looked forward to the Messiah who was to come. Jesus came in a human body as the perfect substitute and lays His life down as the perfect sacrifice for sin.

"He takes away the first in order to establish the second."

It was necessary for the Lord Himself to take away the Old Testament sacrificial system because it was He who established it. But that is what He has done. He has replaced the old system with a wonderfully new and perfect one.

Now let's see what He has guaranteed as a New Testament truth.

Heb.10:10 "By this will we have been sanctified through the offering of the body of Jesus Christ once for all."

Which of your sins does this include? Do you see how many of your sins are paid for? *All!*

How about if I am guilty of hate? Is that paid for? *Yes!*

How about lying? Immorality? Lying? Abortion? Cheating? Stealing?

He paid for each!

You may have done some pretty horrible things. I know I have done things of which I am deeply ashamed. I would be so embarrassed to know that you or someone else had seen me sin. Yet God has seen every time I have sinned and He has seen each of yours. Here is the good news, He died for it all.

How many times does Jesus make this sacrifice? *Once*

How many of your sins are paid for? *All*

Heb. 10:11 Every priest stands daily ministering and offering time after time the same sacrifices, which can never take away sins;

Here the author contrasts the finality of Christ's one perfect sacrifice with the repetition and transitory nature of the priest's sacrifice. Jesus' sacrificial death is not "time after time". It is "Once for all". It takes away all our sin. In your heart of hearts do you truly believe that Jesus' sacrificial death paid for *every* one of your sins? Is there a sin hanging around in your conscience that you feel still stains you? You need to rest in God's Word that Jesus paid for that sin once and for all.

8) <u>Pays for my sin, Past, Present and *Future*</u>

Heb.10:12,13 "but He, having offered one sacrifice for sins <u>for all time</u>, SAT DOWN AT THE RIGHT HAND OF GOD,

Do you see the time frame here? *All time*

Jesus' one perfect sacrifice paid for sins for all time. Next, notice that the Scripture says that after making his sacrifice "He sat down". Why would He do that? The High Priest was never allowed to sit down. Jesus sat down because every requirement had been met. The work was complete. From the cross Jesus says, "It Is Finished." In the Greek that is "Tetelisti"= paid in full.

In light of this, sinners past, present and future who trust in God's wonderful provision of Messiah's sacrifice, no matter in what age they lived, have their sins paid for.

Also, our sin whether it is past, present or yet future is all paid for.

<u>For All Time</u>

<u>PAST</u>	<u>PRESENT</u>	<u>FUTURE</u>
Those O.T. Believers trusted the coming Messiah	*Those living at the time of Jesus*	*We living in who the future*
My Past Sin	*My Present Sin*	*My Future Sin*

Often when I share this truth a person may be able to rest in the promise that his or her past sin is paid for. "But how can my future sin be paid for?" one might ask. I would answer this way, "When Jesus died on Calvary's cross all of your sin was future. He paid for sin for all time."

We are not going to catch Him by surprise when we sin. Can you imagine Jesus saying," Father, did you see what they just did? If We had only known, We would have treated them differently!" He knows every action, good or bad of our whole lives. He took you as His own knowing all about your future. You are safe and secure, totally accepted in His love. He has paid for all your sin past, present and future.

9) <u>I Stand Perfect in God's Eyes</u>

Heb. 10:14 "For by one offering He has perfected for all time those who are sanctified."

• When God looks at an unbeliever, what does He see?

Sin, darkness, rebellion

• When God looks at you Believer, how does He see you?

Perfect, as righteous as Christ

2 Cor.5:21 "He made Him who knew no sin to be sin on our behalf, so that we might become the righteousness of God in Him."

Before Christ when the Lord looked at my heart He saw all my

Thoughts
Words ▶ = Sin = Death "The wages of sin is death."
(Separation from God)
Deeds

Now when the Lord sees me, He does not simply see the debt of my sin cancelled. He now sees me in Christ.

He sees you as perfect as His Son. You look pretty great don't you?

Doesn't that mean that now I could do anything, I could sin all I want? Well, actually, for a true believer the issue is that we sin far more than we want.

There was a British King who wished to review his palace troops. He called the commander of this regiment in and asked him to prepare the men. He wished to have them in their dress uniforms and to have them pass by a particular window where he would be watching. The commander readied his troops and had them march in procession past the king's point of observation. When the king saw the soldiers he became irate. How could this be? If this were some kind of a joke he would demote the person responsible.

He called the commander in. When he reported, the king questioned him. "Whose idea was it," he asked, "to dress the men in white uniforms?" "We are the British! We are the redcoats! What kind of absurd prank is this?"

"Oh Sir, this is not so. I inspected the men myself. Your majesty, they are in red coats," the officer defended.

"Come here to the window and look out and see for yourself!" the king ordered.

The commander walked to the window and to his shock the men did appear to be in white coats. He knew this could not be the case and as he stared out he noticed that there was something unusually different about the window. As he looked closer he realized the window was a stained glass. It was stained a deep red. That is why the coats appeared white.

When one looks at red through a red prism it will appear as white. It is a scientific principle. Look at green through a green prism or yellow through a yellow prism and they will look white. And so it is when God looks at our sin through the blood of His Son, we are thoroughly cleansed, to a pure white.

Isaiah 1:18 "Come let us reason together, says the Lord, though your sins are as scarlet they will be white as snow, though they are red like crimson they will be white like wool."

The Lord has given you, as a believer, the wonderful standing of being utterly clean and pure in standing with Him. We have the righteousness of Christ. We are perfect in His eyes.

10) <u>My sin is absolutely forgiven and forgotten</u>

Heb. 10:15-17 "And the Holy Spirit also testifies to us; for after saying, "THIS IS THE COVENANT THAT I WILL

MAKE WITH AFTER THOSE DAYS, SAYS THE LORD: I WILL PUT MY LAWS UPON THEIR HEART, AND ON THEIR MIND I WILL WRITE THEM," He then says, "AND THEIR SINS AND THEIR LAWLESS DEEDS I WILL REMEMBER NO MORE."

- What does the Lord mean by, "I will remember no more"? *-He has completely forgotten it.*
- If He has done that with your sin what should you do?

God has forgiven and forgotten your sin. He remembers it no more. It is out of His mind, and it is past tense. He acts as if it was never a reality. He never thinks about it when He thinks of you, which is always. He says, "I have forgotten it. I don't remember. It is gone. It is history. Your sins and your lawless deeds I will remember no more."

God is omniscient. He is all knowing. He is so in control of knowledge he can choose to recall or not to recall something. He controls what He remembers. You and I are not able to do that. I am not able to choose to forget anything in particular. I may say I am going to forget something, but I am not able to remove it from my memory. The Lord however is able. He can say He remembers my sin no more because our Lord is so in control of knowledge that He is able to put it out of His thinking. When He thinks of you, your sin is already put away.

Psalm 103:12 He separates our sin from Him, "as far as the East is from the West"

Isaiah 38:17 He places our sin "behind His back". I can't see the small of my back and that is the idea. He places our sin in a place that is not able to be seen.

Micah 7:19 "He casts all of our sin into the "depths of the sea".

Though God says our sin is *forgotten*, in no way are we *forgettable* to God.

Heb. 10:18 "Now where there is forgiveness of these things, there is no longer any offering for sin."

Once one has accepted Christ's forgiveness and sacrifice for one's sins, is there anything else that one must do to be completely forgiven by God? Let me give you a quiz based on the previous verses. Are these statements true or false?

In order to have one's sins forgiven,
one needs to Trust Christ and go to church five times a week.
In order to have one's sins forgiven,
one needs to trust Christ and pray without ceasing.
In order to have one's sins forgiven,
one needs to trust Christ and do penance, expect defeat, be punished, be baptized.
In order to have one's sins forgiven,
one needs to trust Christ and confess sins when one commits them.

No! No! You see there are many who add this last one to what one needs to be forgiven. All I need to have my sins paid for and forgiven is to trust Christ! Is Jesus still seated? *Yes!* (Heb. 10:12) Then Jesus as the perfect High Priest has paid completely for our sin and being finished He sat down.

There is *nothing* I can add to my forgiveness. I simply trust Christ and my sin is completely forgiven. Because He is acceptable and you are in Him, You are as acceptable as Jesus.

Well, then, where does confession fit in? The word confession in the Greek is "Homologia"

Homo = The Same
Logia = Words of, study of

It means to say the same words as God says. What does God say about my sin?

1) He says it is wrong.
2) He says that it is paid for.

3) He says it is forgotten, past, present and future and I stand perfect in His eyes.

So if I say the same words about my sin, I too will say that it is wrong, that Christ has paid for it and then thank Him that I am forgiven. There is nothing I can add to this forgiveness. There is no longer any offering because Christ's offering is full and final.

Heb. 10: 18 "Now where there is forgiveness of these things, there is no longer any offering for sin."

Rest in the righteousness of Christ; you are at peace with God.

11) <u>No Condemnation</u>

Rom.8:1 Therefore there is now no condemnation for those who are in Christ Jesus.

- What does the word "condemnation" mean? To be under adverse judgment, declared to be guilty. To be sentenced to damnation.
- Who might condemn you?

Not God – He has justified you

Rom. 8:30-34 "And those he predestined, he also called; those he called, he also justified; those he justified, he also glorified. What, then, shall we say in response to this? If God is for us, who can be against us? He who did not spare his own Son, but gave him up for us all—how will he not also, along with him, graciously give us all things? Who will bring any charge against those whom God has chosen? It is God who justifies. Who is he that condemns? Christ Jesus, who died—more than that, who was raised to life—is at the right hand of God and is also interceding for us." (NIV)

Self? – In what ways do you condemn yourself?

Others? –What are ways people put expectations on you that leads to your feeling you fall short?

Satan? – He is the enemy of our souls and the accuser of the brethren.

The following are some of the ways we are not to respond: "I'm better than before. I do right things more often now."

That is standing in my self-righteousness. Nor should I mistakenly think that trying to please God can bring greater acceptance. "If I prayed more or witnessed more, then I would be more accepted."

Isaiah 64:6 "All of us have become like one who is unclean and all our righteous acts are like *filthy rags*; we all shrivel up like a leaf, and like the wind our sins sweep us away."

We don't save or display our children's dirty diapers. We dispose of them. When we try to stand before God based on our own goodness it is reveling (showing off) in our dirty diapers.

Let me repeat, "There is no condemnation for those who are in Christ." We are to stand in our imputed righteousness from Christ.

Christianity is God-centered theology not man-centered theology. It focuses on what God has done through Christ not what works man has done. There is nothing that can be done to the sinner to make the sinner any more acceptable to God. Only Jesus is acceptable. I can be as perfectly acceptable as Jesus if I am in Him. When we are born we are in Adam. We are as a result dead in our sins. When we trust Christ we are transferred from being in Adam to being in Christ.

Rom. 5:1, 2 " Therefore, having been justified by faith, we have peace with God through our Lord Jesus Christ, through whom also we have obtained our introduction by faith into this grace in which we stand ; and we exult in hope of the glory of God."

You and I are called to put our faith in what God did through Jesus. Before Christ we had these problems 1) God is holy, 2) We had the debt of our sin, 3) We were in slavery and 4) We were dead.

Notice below we are absent from God's solution. It has all been done by Christ

- Christ is absolutely righteous, satisfying the holiness of God.
- Christ pays the debt of our sin. He died as our substitute.
- Christ purchases our redemption. His blood is the price that buys us out of slavery.
- Christ makes peace and reconciles us to God.

All that is needed for complete forgiveness and acceptance was done through and to Christ. We believe what God did through Christ. Notice, in none of these solutions to our problems before God are we involved. Only Christ and His work have won salvation. When we put our faith in what was done through Christ we are declared righteous and placed into Christ. I am either found in Adam, or I am found in Christ.

Rom. 5:14-16 "Nevertheless, death reigned from the time of Adam to the time of Moses, even over those who did not sin by breaking a command, as did Adam, who was a pattern of the one to come. But the gift is not like the trespass. For if the many died by the trespass of the one man, how much more did God's grace and the gift that came by the grace of the one man, Jesus Christ, overflow to the many! Again, the gift of God is not like the result of the one man's sin: The judgment followed one sin and brought condemnation, but the gift followed many trespasses and brought justification."

If I am in Jesus I am perfect in God's eyes. As an old Imperials song says, "Totally clean before the Lord I stand. In me not one blemish does He see." I am completely forgiven and justified in the righteousness of Christ. God demands a righteousness that is as righteous as His own and that is the free gift He gives us in Christ. Only in Christ can we find the righteousness that satisfies God's Holy nature.

I have watched men and women understand this truth of standing in Christ's righteousness. It enables them to relax and not have to be perfect. The acceptance of the Lord allows them to actually face their sin and see victory. They come to tears as they grasp the freedom that comes with God's grace. It is as if they can feel the Lord's arms wrapped around them as they embrace that they are totally loved and accepted by the Lord.

My life was changed with the realization that God saw me as acceptable as Jesus. In the eyes of the holy God of the universe I was one hundred percent righteous. It was incredible that I was not a stained shameful sinner. I did not have to practice protestant penance. For me that was trying to make up for my sin by being good for a period of time and then I could feel close to the Lord again.

I was wrapped up in my trying to achieve God's favor as opposed to resting in Christ's approval. After I sinned I did not have to wallow in self-pity and guilt. Because I was totally forgiven and had the righteousness of Christ, I could get right back up and with my head in the game.

I have been in basketball games where a player would take a bad shot, the other team would get the rebound, and the guy who took the shot is declaring all the way back down the court, "My bad, my bad." He is not getting back on defense because he is so busy condemning himself. Do you ever hear yourself do that after you have chosen to sin? What do you call yourself? What words do you hear in your mind?

Let me close with this illustration.

Ladies I imagine you thought about your wedding day long before it occurred. That day maybe yet future, but you have imagined it. You have thought about the colors you want or wanted. You have dreamed about the flowers, the music, the reception and the styles of the dresses. You have thought about the atmosphere you desire or desired.

You may have imagined the day of the wedding. You are coming down the aisle to your groom. What do you think is going through his mind as you proceed toward him?

Is he saying, "Girl, why are you wearing your hair like that? You know I don't like it when you wear it that way. Oh, my gosh, that dress does nothing for you. What did you do at the girl's party last night? You look totally spent. Whatever you ate last night has shown up in your complexion today."

No way would he ever think any of those things! I have had the great privilege of performing a number of weddings for dear disciples and have watched the young men as their bride comes down the aisle. They virtually stand in awe!

I can testify personally to this from my own experience when the love of my life came down the aisle. She was radiant. I remember thinking, "Oh my goodness, here she comes! Wow Lord, for me, she's my bride!" The blood drained out of my face. Jan was looking at me, thinking, "Honey, smile it's me." I about passed out. You see, she took my breath away.

That is what I see time and again with these men at their weddings. Their brides take their breath away!

In light of this, look at Col. 1:21, 22

Col. 1:21 "And although you were formerly alienated and hostile in mind, engaged in evil deeds, yet He has now reconciled you in His fleshly body through death, in order to present you before Him holy and blameless and beyond reproach."

Notice this is a *completed* work. He has reconciled us so that we stand before Him holy and blameless with not a single flaw. Now let's compare that to a parallel passage in Eph. 5:25-27

"Husbands, love your wives, just as Christ also loved the church and gave Himself up for her, so that He might sanctify her, having cleansed her by the washing of water with the word, that He might present to Himself the church in all her glory, having no spot or wrinkle or any such thing; but that she would be holy and blameless."

This is how the Lord sees you as His bride, the church. We will stand before Him on that day. We will be presented to Him. There will be no blemishes and no wrinkles. We will be breathtaking in all our glory. Do you get that? You will take Jesus' breath away!

Here is the question you need to answer for yourself, "Do you believe that?" Is this your mindset in your personal times with the Lord walking into His presence or as you meet with Him? Do you believe He sees you as perfectly righteous and that you take His breath away?

Next time you meet with Him picture that reality. Yes, at times we mess up, we sin. But Dear Friend, please know that is not your standing. He sees you as you will look and actually be in heaven. That is our position in Christ. In heaven it will actually be our condition. Now it is our standing in Christ.

Why has He made this true? He wants his people to be secure, to feel fully accepted and close to Him. This leads to our intimacy with Christ. Going back to Hebrews 10, let's see what follows starting in verse 19.

Heb. 10:19-22 "Therefore, brethren, since we have confidence to enter the holy place by the blood of Jesus, by a new and living way which He inaugurated for us through the veil, that is, His flesh, and since we have a great priest over the house of God, let us draw near with a sincere heart in full assurance of faith, having our hearts sprinkled clean from an evil conscience and our bodies washed with pure water."

Let us not sew the veil back up like the Israelites did after the veil in the temple was torn by God, Himself, from top to bottom as a result of the crucifixion. He was visually showing that Jesus the ultimate eternal High Priest had made the way into the Lord's presence ours forever.

Matt. 27:50-51 "And Jesus cried out again with a loud voice, and yielded up His spirit. And behold, the veil of the temple was torn in two from top to bottom; and the earth shook and the rocks were split".

What a remarkable realization! You are personally invited into the Holy of Holies of God's presence. You are deeply loved. He wants you to rest in this truth. You can live in His presence for there is no longer any distance between the Lord and His children. You have complete access. He is inviting you into a deep intimacy. Enjoy being with Him in your personal devotions. Enjoy His presence as you proceed through the activities of each day. Recognize He is sharing the whole experience with you like any father would with his child. Be open, honest and real with Him, sharing your heart.

We are able to draw near to Him. The Holy infinite living God is inviting us into this most personal relationship. Spend time with Him and allow His Word, the Scriptures, to speak to your heart and renew your mind. Walk with Him. His Spirit will illuminate your mind and your conscience. We have a greater privilege than any High Priest of Israel ever experienced. Are you enjoying your salvation and this awesome privilege?

This special relationship affects how we face the challenges in our lives. The Lord wants us to be confident, able to step out in faith, assured we have His favor, never doubting that He is on our side and that he will show up, working to bring about His plan. The Lord does not want us to be fearful in spiritual battle, but to be able to stand strong dressed in His righteousness.

Where has the Lord placed you in His world? What impact would you like to have for His kingdom? What would be a first step? Put that before the Lord and take a step of faith trusting Him to work on your behalf and bring the result you would desire to see.

Sure there will be difficulties along the path as you watch the Lord work as you take one step at time. The difficulties experienced are not because the Lord is displeased with you. He is on your side. He is for you. It is because we live in a fallen world. Like Paul says in Romans 8:31, 32 "If God is for us, who is against us? He who did not spare His own Son, but delivered Him over for us all, how will He not also with Him freely give us all things?"

So in your wonderful standing in Christ you are free to take risks for the Lord knowing you are safe in His acceptance.

POSITIONAL TRUTH SERIES
CHAPTER #3

The <u>Restrainer</u>:

*O*ur next aspect of positional truth to focus on is the ministry of the Holy Spirit (the Restrainer). I feel that it is important to understand and experience the presence and victory that the Holy Spirit provides. The chapter following this we will look at the resources God has given to enable His people to move out into the spiritual battle field of rescuing the perishing.

> 2 Thes. 2:5-8 "Do you not remember that while I was still with you, I was telling you these things? And you know what restrains him now, so that in his time he will be revealed. For the mystery of lawlessness is already at work; only He who now restrains will do so until He is taken out of the way. Then that lawless one will be revealed whom the Lord will slay with the breath of His mouth and bring to an end by the appearance of His coming;"

I am calling the Holy Spirit the Restrainer here because He is the one who is holding back the extent of evil. It is pretty clear what restrains must be a power superior to man and Satan and have a nature totally different to the man of sin. The restraining One is a power and a person. He is the Holy Spirit of God. It is my understanding that prior to the revealing of the Antichrist here called the lawless one, the Holy Spirit and the church will be taken out of the way. He has indwelt His people throughout the church age. As the church is raptured prior to the beginning of the tribulation, He withdraws His presence. Of course God the Holy Spirit is still omnipresent, but His presence will not be manifested in the same manner.

Let's now see how the Holy Spirit impacts positional truth.

D. L. Moody was to have a campaign in England. An elderly pastor protested, "Why do we need this uneducated, inexperienced Mr. Moody? Who does he think he is anyway? Does he think he has a monopoly on the Holy Spirit?" A younger, wiser pastor rose and responded, "No Sir, but the Holy Spirit has a monopoly on Mr. Moody."

The Holy Spirit is able to so work in us. I pray this chapter will give insight as to how this is possible.

12) <u>The Holy Spirit is the gift given (Alas Homas Paracletos)</u>

> 1 Cor. 12:3-7 "...no one can say, "Jesus is Lord," except by the Holy Spirit. Now there are varieties of gifts, but the same Spirit. And there are varieties of ministries, and the same Lord. There are varieties of effects, but the same God who works all things in all persons. But to each one is given the manifestation of the Spirit for the common good."

These manifestations all come from the person of the Holy Spirit who is the special gift to us. He is the gift that came to all believers from the day of Pentecost onward.

In John chapter fourteen, Jesus explains that He is about ready to return to heaven. He explains to His disciples that they should be pleased for Him that He is going back to be with the Father. He is not going to leave them alone but will send the Holy Spirit. He wants them to realize that it is actually better for them that He goes and the Holy Spirit come because He will indwell each of them making them capable of even greater things than He did!

> John 14:16-18 "I will ask the Father, and He will give you another Helper, that He may be with you forever ;that is the

Spirit of truth, whom the world cannot receive, because it does not see Him or know Him, but you know Him because He abides with you and will be in you. "I will not leave you as orphans; I will come to you."

"Another Helper" in the Greek is "αλος 'ομας παρακλετος (alos homas parakletos), Another, Who is exactly the same. If I were to ask someone to get me another pen because the one I am using has run out of ink and do not express specifically what kind of pen, any pen would do. But if I used (Alas Homas), it would mean bring me a silver Parker pen with a fine cartridge. The Father, the Son and the Holy Spirit are each mentioned here in John 14:1-26. Jesus promises us that He and the Father will send the third person of the Trinity, One who is totally equal to each of the other members of the Trinity. We are not alone, for one who is just like Jesus is not only with us, He indwells us. He will manifest Himself in our lives in many ways:

- In changed lives as we display the fruit of the Spirit. (Gal. 5:22, 23)
- In the spiritual gift we express as we serve. (1 Cor. 12:7-11)
- In the empowerment he gives the new nature. (putting off the old nature sinful action and putting on the new nature activity). (Eph. 4:22-24)
- In the power He gives as we go out as witnesses. (Acts 1:8)
- In our ablity to understand the Scriptures as He illuminates our minds. (1 Cor. 2:10-16)
- In confirming in our spirit that we are children of God. (Rom. 8:16)
- IN helping us to pray by interceding, expressing our deepest longings. (Rom. 8:26,27)
- In the power to live godly lives. (Christlikeness) 2 Cor. 3:18)

Jesus has promised The Holy Spirit, Who is the gift.

13) He indwells us

He, the third person of the Trinity, indwells each believer. The believer's heart is His home. He is the one who quickens us. We are spiritually alive because of Him. As a result of this new birth and His indwelling presence there is now *the new you!* This new you is *the real you*. Jesus told the disciples to stay in Jerusalem until they received the Holy Spirit, then they would have power. Unless one is indwelt by the Holy Spirit, one is not a child of God as the following verse explains.

> Rom. 8:9-11 "However, you are not in the flesh but in the Spirit, if indeed the Spirit of God dwells in you. But if anyone does not have the Spirit of Christ, he does not belong to Him. If Christ is in you, though the body is dead because of sin, yet the spirit is alive because of righteousness."

In the Old Covenant the Spirit would come upon believers for a time and then He would leave. An example would be that he came upon messengers of Saul and Saul himself who prophesized and then He left them. (1 Sam. 19:20-25) David even prays regarding this. "Do not cast me away from your presence and do not take Your Holy Spirit from me."(Ps. 51:11)

Jesus tells us in (John 14:16-20) that the Spirit will now be in us and it is not a temporal residence but a permanent one.

> "That is the Spirit of truth, whom the world cannot receive, because it does not see Him or know Him, but you know Him because He abides with you and will be in you." John 14:17

Let me share this quote from an unknown source. It fits well with this area of positional truth. "When the Spirit comes and indwells a believer, He makes Christ dearer, heaven nearer and the Word of God clearer." Being indwelt by the Spirit we are the dwelling place of God's presence on earth, and as the Scripture states, we are literally the temple of God. You carry with you wherever you go the presence of God. Because we are the dwelling place of the Holy Spirit we represent Him in whatever we do and wherever we go.

> 1 Cor. 3:16, 17 "Do you not know that you are a temple of God and that the Spirit of God dwells in you? If any man

destroys the temple of God, God will destroy him, for the temple of God is holy, and that is what you are."

I was so delighted recently when doing business with a very over-whelmed retail clerk. It was obvious it had been a difficult day and now with my particular order things had gotten even more messed up. It was ending in frustrating delays and added expense. The woman waiting on me looked up at me and said, "What is it with you? You are being so patient and understanding and nice. Don't get me wrong, I appreciate it, but that's not normal." I smiled and said, "Thank you I think, but you know I think this is how Jesus would treat you. So my hope is you see Him through me."

14) <u>The Holy Spirit fills every yielded life</u>

Eph. 5:18 "And do not get drunk with wine, for that is excessive, but be filled with the Spirit,"

Be filled with the Spirit. This is a command for every believer. Being filled with the Spirit is to be the norm in the Christian life. The command in the original language would translate, "Be ye being filled." That is a continual ongoing process. It is not a once and for all thing.

Maybe you can relate to my life when I first learned to walk with the Lord. It seemed like every time I turned around I was saying, "I'm sorry God, and I feel bad about what I did." "Oh, I'm sorry God, I did it again." "I'm sorry God, I am so bad." I knew I was going the wrong direction, but I didn't know how to get turned around.

It was like an experience I had in a strange city. It was night and I was lost and as a result I turned left onto a four lane, one way street with traffic coming straight at me, headlights shining in my eyes. Panic struck me, "I'm going to die and take a few people with me." I needed to get out of the dilemma, but how?

I pulled over the curb onto a sidewalk with my headlights boring into the front window of a busy restaurant. I had escaped death, but now what? A very patient and gracious police officer found me a few minutes later. He gave me directions to my destination and actually directed traffic so I could back out and be on my way, this time in the right direction.

That is what I needed to know when it came to my struggle to please God with my life. How do I get turned around in my spiritual life? How do I turn from sin and start walking with God?

First, I needed to recognize that the direction I was going was wrong and self-destructive. I needed to confess and turn (repent). Next, I needed to obey God's command and be filled with the Spirit. We refer to this as spiritual breathing. Exhale is confessing one's sin and inhaling is appropriating the filling of the Holy Spirit. I am able to ask God to fill me and to be certain that I am filled because of His promise in 1 John 5:14, 15.

Since the Lord has commanded us to be filled with the Spirit, we know that it is His will. Since it is His will, when we ask Him to fill us we have the assurance that he will do it.

1John 5: 14, 15 "And this is the confidence which we have before Him, that, if we ask anything according to His will, He hears us. And if we know that He hears us in whatever we ask, we have the requests which we have asked from Him."

Tony Evans has explained that not being Spirit filled is that spiritual state where a born-again Christian knowingly and persistently lives to please and serve self rather than Christ. The same kind of things you would not be surprised to find with just ordinary people, you will find are true of these Christians who are not living in their new nature. They are living just like ordinary people. They are not living up to or experiencing their potential. We have often said the believer who is not walking in the Spirit is the most miserable of people because he is going against his true self.

If you are not sure you are filled with the Spirit, you can appropriate His filling first by talking with the Lord to see if there is any unconfessed sin in your life. Second, is yield to God's command to be filled, and lastly, claim His promise from 1 John 5:14, 15.

In one of his meetings, D.L. Moody was explaining to his audience the truth that we cannot bring about spiritual changes in our lives by our own strength. He demonstrated the principal like this:

"Tell me," he said to his audience, "how can I get the air out of the tumbler I have in my hand?" One man said, "Suck it out with a pump." But Moody replied, "That would create a vacuum and shatter it." Finally after many suggestions, he picked up a pitcher and quietly filled the glass with water. "There," he said, "all the air is now gone from this tumbler. He then went on to explain that victory in the Christian life is not accomplished by "sucking out a sin here and there," but by being filled with the Holy Spirit.

To be filled with the Spirit is also to be emptied of self. Our goal is not to be introspective trying to rid ourselves of sin, but to be occupied with Christ and we will be transformed to be more like Him.

In Galatians 5:16, it says, "Walk in the Spirit and you will not carry out the desire of the flesh". As you walk in the Spirit He is illuminating your mind. The Spirit will be illuminating your conscience and will be developing conviction points. You may be in the midst of a behavior or action in response to some temptation. The Holy Spirit will touch your thoughts and in your mind you will hear, "Child of mine, what are you doing? That is sin, don't do that". If you agree with the Lord and *turn at that conviction point*; you continue to be filled with the Spirit and are *walking in the light*. If you *do not turn* but continue to *carry out* the desire of the flesh, you are no longer filled with the Spirit. It is here where 1 John 1:9 needs to be applied, when it says,

> "If we (confess) say openly that we have done wrong (to the Lord), He is upright and true to His word, giving us forgiveness of sins and making us clean from all evil.(Bible in Basic English)"

To be filled with the Spirit again I need to confess that sin and yield again to the Spirit's control. As you grow in the Lord your conviction points will come sooner and you will hear in your mind the Spirit's prompting even before you begin an action or begin to yield to a temptation. You can picture this like two lines that start out a good distance apart but narrow as you grow. The end target that you are moving toward is Christ. The more you grow, the closer the conviction points come together.

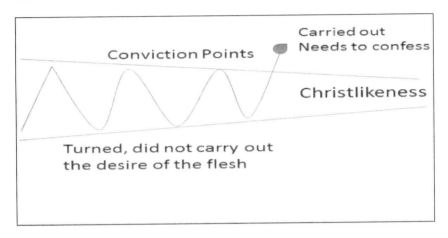

Because you are walking in the light you become more aware of those things in your life that are not pleasing the Lord. If a man in a perfectly white T-shirt were to enter a coal mine. He would not be aware of the dust that was collecting on his white clothes until he stepped out again into the light. That is like us. When we start walking with the Lord we step into the light and we now become aware of things in our lives under the scrutiny of the Spirit that need changing.

The Lord teaches us how to walk with Him moment by moment with other concepts in Scripture such as: abiding in Christ (John 15). Here the picture of abiding in the vine is the idea of being attached to, yielded to the true source of nourishment and life. The believer is obedient to Christ's commands and a follower of the Word of God. As a believer abides in the Lord, the Lord prunes those areas in his life that hinder growth.

Being filled with the Spirit is also related to the concept of walking in the light (1John 1:5-10). God Himself is light and as we walk in His light we have fellowship with Him at the same time, and Christ's sacrificial blood cleanses us from all our sins.

Living in your new nature (Eph.4:24) is coupled with putting off the old man actions and putting on the new man actions, (Eph. 4:22-24), and is also related to the filling of the Holy Spirit. We will look at this again in the next chapter with positional truth #24.

15) <u>He baptizes us into Christ (Placing us into the body of Christ)</u>

1 Cor. 12:13 "For by one Spirit we were all baptized into one body, whether Jews or Greeks, whether slaves or free, and we were all made to drink of one Spirit."

The Spirit identifies the believer with all that it means to be in Christ.

The old nature is circumcised off the real you.
We are dead to sin and separated from the old nature.
The old nature is still in this body of death.
These two are in me, but only the new nature is attached to me.

Rom. 6:9-11 "For we know that since Christ was raised from the dead, he cannot die again; death no longer has mastery over him. The death he died, he died to sin once for all; but the life he lives, he lives to God. In the same way, count yourselves dead to sin but alive to God in Christ Jesus."

When we reckon or count on something we accept it as an accomplished fact. The word "baptize" means to "dip," "to plunge," "to immerse." Our identity is changed by our union with Christ. We are now identified as Christians, and members of Christ's body of believers. We are no longer in old Adam's family. We have a new family with a new identity; Christ is the head of our new family.

When you trusted Christ the old nature was declared legally dead and was circumcised off the real you (Col.2:11). The old nature, though it is still in this body of death, is no longer attached to the real you. You were baptized into Christ and buried with Christ positionally, separated from the old nature, legally and actually. As explained in the first chapter, when something is dead in Scripture it is separated from what it is dead to. If one is dead one is separated from and unresponsive to stimuli. In Galatians 5:24 we are told, "We have crucified the flesh with its evil passions and desires." I was dead to God. Now I am dead to sin.

Look with me to Colossian 2:11-14

Col. 2:11-14 "In him you were also circumcised, in the putting off of the sinful nature, not with a circumcision done by the hands of men but with the circumcision done by Christ, having been *buried with him in baptism* and raised with him through your faith in the power of God, who raised him from the dead. When you were dead in your sins and in the uncircumcision of your sinful nature, God made you alive with Christ. He forgave us all our sins, having canceled the written code, with its regulations, that was against us and that stood opposed to us; he took it away, nailing it to the cross". (NIV)

I am alive. I am forgiven. Yet there still is a battle with the flesh. What is this "Old Nature"? What happened to my "Old Nature" at conversion?

The "old nature" is "the sin nature", "my old self", "my old man and "the flesh". These are all descriptions of the same spiritual issue. It is not just old habits. It is as described in Romans 7:17 "sin which indwells me." Romans 8:3-8 explains that there is a law of sin and death at work in the old nature. The old nature is opposed to the Spirit. My flesh cannot please God because it is hostile toward God. God does not retread or improve the old. The old man, what I was prior to Christ as a natural man, is so incorrigibly corrupt that even God Himself does not attempt to improve it, fix it, repair or reform it. He regards the old nature as being absolutely hopeless. So He creates a *brand new thing*, it is the new creation, the *new man*.

Galatians 5:17 further explains that the flesh, "the sinful nature, desires what is contrary to the Spirit, and the Spirit desires what is contrary to the sinful nature. They are in conflict with each other, so that you do not do what you want." (NIV) There is a drive in my heart toward self and selfishness to indulge the flesh.

In 1 John 2:16 this is emphasized as "The lust of the flesh and the lust of the eyes and the boastful pride of life." The flesh can be aroused. It can be inflamed. It is not merely old habits or poor thinking. The flesh will come to attention and react to temptation.

For example, you are very content with the car you are driving. It gets you places just fine. Then a friend shows up with this brand spanking new car with all the bells and whistles. You sit in it and that new car smell draws you in. You can't afford it, but you want one. Where does the desire come from? There is this longing, a hunger to satisfy. You think to yourself, "I am less without this car." If I had one of these my life would be really, really fulfilled. Where did that feeling come from? That's the flesh.

Eph. 4:22-24 "that, in reference to your former manner of life, you lay aside the old self, which is being *corrupted* in accordance with the lusts of deceit, and that you be renewed in the spirit of your mind, and *put* on the *new self*, which in the likeness of God has been created in righteousness and holiness of the truth."

The Scripture teaches:

- The old nature is still in this body of death. (Romans 7:24)
- It is still being corrupted. (Eph. 4:22)

There are actions or thoughts that are in accordance with the old nature. There are new nature thoughts and actions. As you put on or steps into new nature action or thought, the Spirit of God empowers you. This is where the new you belongs and actually in your heart of hearts desires to be. To Paul it is unthinkable that a Christian would want to continue in the old way of life. Would a man rescued from a concentration camp want to go back to its torture and terror? Why would a leper who has been healed and thoroughly cleansed and bathed put back on his leper's rags?

Sin is so horrible God executed my Adamic nature. He separated me from it. Why would those who have been freed from sin want to continue under its tyranny and power? Sin is serious stuff. God hates it so much, He died for it! So did you because you were placed in Him at salvation.

Sin finds its source in the will, but uses the body as an instrument. The sinful desire originates with the evil nature, not the physical body. My sinful nature is an intangible, invisible entity; it is not able to be observed, so I cannot guard against it. So the believer is told and is able to keep watch over the members of his body, i.e., what the mind thinks about, what the eye looks at, what the ear listens to, what the hands do and the feet carry him to.

Actually it is more than that. Not what ears hear, but what they listen to. Not what eyes see, but what they look at. Not what has your attention for a moment or what merely passes through the mind, but what do I engage in my mind? We carry on conversations in our minds. Sometimes we need to change the subject, change the conversation we are dwelling on. As new creations we can do that!

> Romans 6:13 "Do not offer the parts of your body to sin, as instruments of wickedness, *(Put off the old man sin)* but rather offer yourselves to God, *(Put on the new man righteous action or thought)* as those who have been brought from death to life; and offer the parts of your body to him as instruments of righteousness." (NIV) *Words in parentheses are my addition*

The word "instruments" is a military term. It would be better translated by the word weapons. It would be foolish for a man to turn over his armaments to his enemy. But that is precisely what you do when you yield parts of your body to sin as opposed to righteousness. We hinder the progress of the kingdom. We are inviting the enemy to use us for his purposes. We are engaging in friendly fire.

When I present my body as an instrument of righteousness, the Holy Spirit empowers me to righteous action. I am living as my new heart desires.

> *Ezekiel 36:26* "Moreover I will give you a new heart and put a new spirit with in you; and I will remove the heart of stone from your flesh and give you a heart of flesh." (*One that is alive to God*)

You and I are in a war. It is serious when we surrender the members of our body to sin. Believer, consider the members of your earthly body as dead to immorality. Yield them to God. You can because the Spirit has baptized you with Christ and you died to sin.

16) <u>The Holy Spirit Seals Us in the Lord</u>

The Spirit of God Himself, the Holy Spirit of promise, is given to us. He has been given to us, as a down payment, a pledge of our inheritance of all that is to come, as a taste of heaven. He seals us in Christ as found in Eph. 1:13, 14.

> Eph. 1:13,14 "In Him, you also, after listening to the message of truth, the gospel of your salvation -having also believed, you were sealed in Him with the Holy Spirit of promise, who is given as a pledge of our inheritance, with a view to the redemption of God's own possession, to the praise of His glory".

The Holy Spirit is God's down payment on all that is true now by faith and will be true by sight in heaven. We put earnest money down on a house to demonstrate our sincere intention of following through on buying it. A woman is given an engagement ring by her fiancé as his show of love and to demonstrate his promise to marry. When the Lord seals us in Christ and gives us His Holy Spirit, as a pledge of our inheritance, we have a wonderful picture of the security of our salvation. How could we lose our salvation? The Lord would never forfeit the Holy Spirit. God has sealed His promise by giving us Himself.

This sealing is also illustrated by God in John 10:1-29. No one can snatch us out of either the Father or the Son's hand.

> "and I give eternal life to them, and they will never perish; and no one will snatch them out of My hand. "My Father, who has given them to Me, is greater than all; and no one is able to snatch them out of the Father's hand." John 10:28, 29

We are sealed by the Spirit and held tightly in the Father and the Son's grasp. Now that's security.

17) <u>We have the mind of Christ; He illuminates our minds to know the Word</u>

1 Cor. 2:10, 11 For to us God revealed them through the Spirit; for the Spirit searches all things, even the depths of God. (We can be men and women of the Word). Now we have received, not the spirit of the world, but the Spirit who is from God, so that we may know the things freely given to us by God...:16 we have the mind of Christ." — *Words in parentheses are my addition*

Col .3:16" Let the word of Christ richly dwell within you, with all wisdom teaching and admonishing one another with psalms and hymns and spiritual songs, singing with thankfulness in your hearts to God."

- The Holy Spirit illuminates our minds to understand God's Word.
- The Word feeds our spiritual hearts and renews our minds.
- The Spirit calls to mind the Word that we have hid in our hearts as we walk with Him.
- We can understand the Word and we hunger and long to spend time in it.

Far too many consider the Christian life as dull, mindless, pointless, silly, out of touch with reality, and intellectually without credibility. They have concluded that our faith is filled with endless restraints of do's and don'ts. If they only knew that it is the most thrilling, challenging, fulfilling and enriching life that the human spirit can experience they would be beating down the doors to get in. All this and a relationship with our precious Savior await them.

This is the best stuff. It is certainly not boring. We have been let in on the mind of God, The divine mind, the very depths of God Himself. What is being revealed to us is that God is He who is endless, eternal, omnipresent and inscrutable. We are let into His ways, His attributes and His plans. Because of the Holy Spirit you are able to understand His revelation in the Word of God.

1 Cor. 2:14-15a "A natural man does not accept the things of the Spirit of God, for they are foolishness to him; and he cannot understand them, because they are spiritually appraised. But he who is spiritual appraises all things",

18) <u>Because we are now spiritual; we exhibit the fruit of the Spirit.</u>

To understand our spirituality let's look further at the struggle that exists between the Spirit and the flesh as Paul teaches in Galatians 5:16-25

Gal. 5:16-18 "But I say, walk by the Spirit, and you will not carry out the desire of the flesh. For the flesh sets its desire against the Spirit, and the Spirit against the flesh; for these are in opposition to one another, so that you may not do the things that you please. But if you are led by the Spirit, you are not under the Law."

Notice the flesh has a desire, and is not just a habit. Romans 7:17 teaches, "It is sin which indwells me." Sin comes to life and our flesh is seduced, it is attracted to the sin action. The Lord has made the fruit of the Spirit natural to our new nature. We are to abide, not to squeeze out these qualities by our self-effort.

Ben Franklin tried to improve his life and to live a perfect life. He decided to add a virtue each day until he reached the level of moral perfection he desired. He started with a first virtue, added a second, but found by the third he was already failing with the first. He found his quest impossible to achieve. There is only one person who has lived the perfect life and that is Jesus. If I want to live a victorious Christian life I have to live in the power of the Holy Spirit. I need to abide in Christ. It is humanly impossible without Him.

The fruit of the Spirit.

Gal 5:22-25 "But the fruit of the Spirit is love, joy, peace, patience, kindness, goodness, faithfulness, gentleness, self-control; against such things there is no law. Now those who belong to Christ Jesus have crucified the flesh with its passions and desires. If we live by the Spirit, let us also walk by the Spirit."

We are spiritual and the fruit of the Spirit is the natural life for us. The real you is behaving in character when you live out the fruit of the Spirit. Now as I mature and have my mind renewed these qualities grow. Believer you are one who is loving. You are kind. You are faithful. Yes, you are patient. This is true of the new you. The Lord works in your life and the expression of these qualities mature.

Picture your life as a plate of glass. The Lord etches the character of Christ into your life through His Word. Picture a portion of the glass being cut. Then He uses the challenges you face the difficulties and trials in life to knock on the glass and tink, tink, tink right where Jesus has been etched the piece falls and more of the character of our Lord is revealed.

As Paul explains legalism cannot produce fruit any more than hanging an apple on a thorn bush can change the thorn bush into an apple tree. You as a believer are spiritual. To be in character we are patient, kind, good and faithful. Think of the difference between a moldy piece of fruit and one freshly picked. Displaying the fruit of the Spirit we are like a freshly picked apple in an orchard on a cool fall day. You take a bite and the crispness of the bite echoes in the morning air. The juice rolls down your cheek. It is utterly satisfying and desirable like the fruit of the Spirit.

I belong to Jesus. Since that is true, here is what follows, I have a crucified flesh. It has been executed, dead. Since these qualities are true of the real me in my heart of hearts, a question follows. Am I living in character or out of character?

As I yield my true self, the real me, to the control and power of the Holy Spirit. The fruit of the Spirit is being produced and displayed in my life not by the law but by abiding in Christ. This illustration helps me with the "how" of that abiding by yielding to the Spirit.

Picture with me what it is like to move a motorless boat through the water. One option is for it to be moved by the currents, waves and tides. You might eventually wash up on some shore. One is vulnerable and dependent upon outside influences. There are believers who are tossed to and fro by circumstances. If life is going well and things are working out, they might feel close to the Lord. Each may think, "I have a good relationship with my significant other; therefore God is good." If life is throwing one a tough time one could feel far from the Lord. The pressures come, bad circumstances hit, and trials drag the person down into struggle. In this case the Christian life and one's happiness is dependent upon what happens to the individual.

A second way a boat could be moved through the water is by rowing it with oars. This is getting to a destination through the sweat and strain of one's own strength. We can try to live the Christian life in our own strength. This way is gutting it out, gritting my teeth and trying to make it on my own. This is not what the Lord intended and it never works.

A third way to see that boat moved is by hoisting the sails and submitting to the power and direction of the wind. For the believer the Holy Spirit, who is the dearest real and alive person, is waiting for us to depend on Him and yield to Him. As the wind directs and empowers a sail boat, the Holy Spirit guides and empowers a believer. This is how I go in the right direction. As one abides in Christ and is yielded to the Spirit, the fruit of the Spirit and the true person that you are becomes more and more evident.

19) <u>The Spirit gives to each believer at least one spiritual gift.</u>

1 Cor. 12:1 "Now concerning spiritual gifts, brethren, I do not want you to be unaware."

We find the different lists of gifts in four places throughout the New Testament. Romans 12: 4-13, Eph. 4:5-16, 1 Peter 4:10, 11 as well as the chief passage here in chapters 12 through 14 of first Corinthians. We each have received at least one spiritual gift. What we want to look at is the reason the Lord has given us these gifts.

Paul, in order to explain this truth, uses a visual illustration. We all have one of his examples with our own bodies. We see how our bodies have many parts but they all work together and act as one person.

Another example to help us see this is an orchestra. There are strings, brass, percussion and woodwinds in an orchestra. All are played differently and each produces different sounds. Together they harmonize and create beautiful music.

If we will function as a body the world will know that God is in the midst of His people. Jesus is present through His Spirit. *He manifests His presence through us as He has gifted us.* We are His hands, his feet, his eyes, His voice and His heart.

He, the Holy Spirit, is the distributor of the spiritual gifts.

1 Cor. 12:18-20 "But now God has placed the members, each one of them, in the body, just as He desired. If they were all one member, where would the body be? But now there are many members, but one body."

The variations in the functions of the body are handpicked. The Lord custom builds and with those variations actually increase the ability of the body of Christ to have impact for the Kingdom. The arrangement of the body is not by chance, but is due to the Spirit's ordering.

1 Cor. 12:11, 12 "But one and the same Spirit works all these things, distributing to each one individually just as He wills. For even as the body is one and yet has many members, and all the members of the body, though they are many, are one body, so also is Christ."

The Holy Spirit manifests His presence differently in each believer. The purpose of these gifts is for the common good. You need me. I need you. You are going to be different from me. I am going to be different from you. No one believer can do it all. You cannot do it all; you need the rest of the body. Every gift is important or the Lord would not give it. We are to appreciate our own gift and to use it as a good steward. We are not to depreciate any gift or member of the body.

Ever go to the beach and get sand in an eye? A few little specks of sand does so much damage it feels like you are totally incapacitated. I remember having this happen to me. I couldn't stop blinking and the eye just watered continuously. I put a patch over it hoping to kind of isolate the problem. It didn't help. The nagging pain made me nauseous and weak. Finally it gave me a headache and distorted my vision. I dropped things. I spilled things. As a result of all that I stubbed my toe. I virtually hurt from head to toe. That night I was supposed to continue a series from the book of Ephesians. Try to read or share a message when you can't see clearly. One little scratch in my eye and my whole body sympathized and suffered. You received a spiritual gift at salvation and the whole body of Christ will benefit as you exercise it or suffer if you don't.

20) <u>The One who comes with strength empowers us for evangelism "The Paracletos"</u>

Acts 1:8 "but you will receive power when the Holy Spirit has come upon you; and you shall be My witnesses both in Jerusalem, and in all Judea and Samaria, and even to the remotest part of the earth."

I heard R.C. Sproul speak at a conference in Pittsburgh my first year in the ministry. He shared some concepts that related to the Holy Spirit that revolutionized my understanding and confidence in stepping out in faith in evangelism. He defined the meaning of the Greek word "Paracletos" which is interpreted as Helper, Advocate or Comforter in various Bible translations.

John 16:7-13 "But I tell you the truth, it is to your advantage that I go away ; for if I do not go away, the Helper will not come to you; but if I go, I will send Him to you. "And He, when He comes, will convict the world concerning sin and righteousness and judgment; concerning sin, because they do not believe in Me; and concerning righteousness, because I go to the Father and you no longer see Me; and concerning judgment, because the ruler of this world has been judged. "I have many more things to say to you, but you cannot bear them now. "But when He, the Spirit of truth, comes, He will guide you into all the truth;

He explained that the Paraclete is more than one who consoles or counsels. He certainly does that but in the culture from which John is writing the Paracletos was an attorney who was retained with an abiding fee. He was a family advocate who was bound by honor, integrity and position to stand by his humble client to the end. He is to be attentive in interceding for any member of the family in need. He is the one called alongside to defend.

Jesus said in John 14:7 "It is to your advantage that I go! If I do not go the Holy Spirit will not come to indwell you."

"Do you believe" Dr. Sproul inquired of us, "that it was better that Jesus go?' He went on to explain that it is one thing to go out in the name of Jesus who does some pretty neat stuff and is a great preacher. It is quite another to go indwelt by the Spirit of the living Christ who has conquered death and is reigning as King of the Universe in Heaven." Dr. Sproul shared that the King James translation used the word "comforter" because at the time of its translation the Latin language was a predominant influence. In Latin we have "comforter" coming from the words "Cum Forte", meaning He is the One who comes "with strength". He is not passively standing by patting us on the head when we get bruised or beat up. No. He is actively involved with us in the battle.

Jesus is our advocate before the Father. The Holy Spirit is our advocate before the world.

> 1 John 2:1 "My little children, I am writing these things to you so that you may not sin. And if anyone sins, we have an Advocate with the Father, Jesus Christ the righteous;"

There is no context for evangelism without truth. We have the Spirit of truth. He is the one who convicts of sin, righteousness and judgment. Again this is a tremendous environment for evangelism. The Holy Spirit does not allow the Word of God to return void but convicts the heart of the person with whom we share the gospel.

What a great confidence this can lead to for us. We can expect the Lord to work mightily when we step out in faith and take the initiative to share Him with others. Dr. Sproul shared with us the following verses as he brought his message to a close. He was calling us to believe God for great impact. He emphasized the victory God spells out here in Romans eight.

> Romans 8:32-37 "He who did not spare His own Son, but delivered Him over for us all, how will He not also with Him freely give us all things? Who will bring a charge against God's elect? God is the one who justifies; who is the one who condemns? Christ Jesus is He who died, yes, rather who was raised, who is at the right hand of God, who also intercedes for us. Who will separate us from the love of Christ? Will tribulation, or distress, or persecution, or famine, or nakedness, or peril, or sword? Just as it is written, "FOR YOUR SAKE WE ARE BEING PUT TO DEATH ALL DAY WE WERE CONSIDERED AS SHEEP TO BE SLAUGHTERED. *But in all these things we overwhelmingly conquer through Him who loved us."*

This is not the picture of a battered and exhausted victor, but rather a confident and triumphant conqueror. I believe it is our holy God getting credit for victory. In the might of Christ we have become overwhelming conquerors. That thought ought to lead us to attempt the heroic as the church. We ought to be standing in the classroom, at our place of work and in our neighborhoods expectant that God will show up and bring all of Himself to bear. I came away from the time with Dr. Sproul where he helped me to think, "We ought not to be hesitant as if Egypt was behind us causing us to tremble in fear. We need not feel helpless with the sea in front of us, that sea of prebelievers who are in desperate need of knowing our Savior for the Spirit of truth will convict their heart. Nor should we cower because there are mountains of difficult problems towering over us on either side like huge barriers." It does not depend on how overwhelming or intimidating my immediate supervisor is. Nor does it matter the professor's intellect. Not even the sense of how insurmountable my challenges may appear. We are going into these steps of faith with the Holy Spirit. You and I have one who comes, "cum-forte", with strength.

We need men and women like Moses standing up and saying, "Behold the hand of God, the salvation of the Lord," stretching forth the rod of God and watching the sea part. We move forth conquering in the name of Christ, believing God. Is it possible? What is to stop us? This is ours because we are in Christ accompanied by Him who indwells us.

Let us dream. Let us be His people who watch Him work mightily. Oh Lord, conquer through us. What is it that the Lord has laid upon your heart? Trust Him and step out in faith and go for it!

Brethren we are living in the most exciting time ever. That is not hype. That is not a bias to our time in history. That is reality. You and I literally have the opportunity to see the whole planet reached with the gospel.

Forty things happened to you the instant you became a Christian. They affect your relationship and intimacy with the Lord. They affect your standing and acceptance by the Lord. They also affect your moment by moment walk, victory and witness for the Lord.

The next three chapters will help you realize that God has provided you with the resources to go for those dreams he has placed on your heart and enable you to move forward in His Great Commission.

POSITIONAL TRUTH SERIES
CHAPTER #4

———⌇⌇———

So far we have looked at the truths of our position in Christ, first these that affect our *relationship* and intimacy with the Lord. Being alive spiritually we are able to have a relationship with the living God. Our relationship is further enhanced because we belong to Him as His children. How wonderfully close this relationship is. Christ literally indwells us.

Second is our standing in His *righteousness*. We are able to draw near because we are thoroughly accepted in the Beloved. We are as acceptable as the Lord is Himself. We have been given as a gift the very righteousness of God. This is a wonderful security. Being this safe with the Lord we are confident that He is completely on our side. Now as sons and daughters of the king we see ourselves through our Lord's eyes. We can also see the world and the people who dwell here from the Lord's perspective.

Because of the Holy Spirit, you and I are able to walk in His light. We have His power and presence. He has made living the Christian life possible. As part of our position in Christ, we are empowered and defended before the world as witnesses by the Holy Spirit. This may be a daily battle for us as we remind ourselves of these truths.

Most of us as we become believers do so because we have sensed our need. We felt the guilt of our sin and wanted the forgiveness Jesus offers. We came to Christ because we wanted to go to heaven. Our motive was "Jesus loves me this I know for the Bible tells me so".

Later as we grow as believers we lift our eyes and see that salvation is offered to everyone and become others-centered. Our focus is on a world of people who need to hear that message. We have progressed from its all about me to no, it is about others. Ultimately we grow to see that all the Lord has done he has been done to His glory and as we are involved in His purposes we can bring Him glory.

> 2 Cor. 5:14, "For Christ's love compels us, because we are convinced that one died for all, and therefore all died. And he died for all, that those who live should <u>no longer live for themselves</u> <u>but for him</u> who died for them and was raised again." (NIV)

We need to see ourselves differently. We are to see the needs of the world and how the Lord has positioned us and given us His *resources* to be His ambassadors. That is our call as expressed here by Paul.

> 2 Cor. 5:20 "Therefore, we are ambassadors for Christ, as though God were making an appeal through us; we beg you on behalf of Christ, be reconciled to God".

A believer goes from being self-centered to Christ-centered as our view of God grows, our view of positional truth grows and our eternal perspective grows.

<u>Resources</u>

We are called to be involved in God's eternal purposes. We are ambassadors given the command to go and tell all peoples the good news of what Jesus has accomplished and what He offers to every person. This is a huge challenge and responsibility. When the Lord sends us into the world He has completely provided all the resources needed to fulfill this commission, The Great Commission. The first three aspects of our position have spoken to very real needs we have to be whole people. The intimacy of our relationship spoke to our need for belonging and we belong to the Father as His children. Jesus makes us worthy as we have been imputed His very righteousness giving us wonderful security. The Holy Spirit through His power and guidance makes us capable. We know that the Lord is for us and that He will show up.

The next three aspects of positional truth (Resources, Rights, and Regality) help us understand why Paul can say we are more than conquerors. We are supplied with all the resources necessary to enter into this tremendous spiritual endeavor to win the lost for Christ. We will encounter obstacles and spiritual battle and need to understand the resources the Lord has provided for us to overcome these, even to face the enemy himself. Let's look at just a few of the verses that promise us great victory.

Rom. 8:31, 32 "What then shall we say to these things? If God is for us, who is against us? He who did not spare His own Son, but delivered Him over for us all, how will He not also with Him freely give us all things"?

8:37 "But in all these things we overwhelmingly conquer through Him who loved us."

Eph. 6:10-12 "Finally, be strong in the Lord and in the strength of His might. Put on the full armor of God, so that you will be able to stand firm against the schemes of the devil. For our struggle is not against flesh and blood, but against the rulers, against the powers, against the world forces of this darkness, against the spiritual forces of wickedness in the heavenly places."

In this aspect of our position we are going to look at six more of the truths of our position in Christ. I have a call as a believer. That call is to be involved in the Great Commission our Lord gave us in addresses to His disciples before His ascension. Here is just one from Matthew.

"Then Jesus came to them and said, "All authority in heaven and on earth has been given to me. Therefore go and make disciples of all nations, baptizing them in the name of the Father and of the Son and of the Holy Spirit, and teaching them to obey everything I have commanded you. And surely

I am with you always, to the very end of the age." Matthew 28:18-20 (NIV)

The Lord does not expect you and me to participate in this great challenge by our own resources or means. The Christian life is not meant to be lived in our own strength, nor are we expected to see the kingdom move forward on meager rations. Forty things happened to you the instant you became a Christian, but it seems at times we are just getting by. We do not feel the need to live in our position. Maybe it is because the Christian life has become a routine? Many times it is because we are not stepping out in faith looking to see the gospel go forward. Are we just living for the things of today not for that which is eternal?

This makes me think of the story of the California miner. He lived in an old shack close to the streams where he panned for gold and the cave that he steadily worked hoping to strike a vein. There was a stove and a single bed and a cupboard to store his food and not much else in the old place. This nice old gentleman had been a prospector for nearly forty years. Folks liked him and enjoyed the stories he'd share when he would come into town for supplies. It seemed he could eke out enough specks of gold for himself and his old burro to get by. He said he didn't need much else. A number of days had passed and no one had seen the old guy. So a couple of men from the town went out to the shack to look in on him. They found him stretched out on his meager cot motionless, dead. It appeared that he had passed away quietly in the night. They buried him just a few feet behind his shack. Well, when they dug a hole an amazing thing happened. They discovered what turned out to be the richest gold strike in the history of California. The old man had been sitting on it the whole time!

You and I can be like that miner! We have the riches of our position in Christ, the resources enable us to take the good news to the frontlines. We don't realize all that is ours and we eke out an existence as believers as if we were paupers and we fail to advance the gospel. All the time we are sitting on the vast resources that are available to us if we would draw on them. The Lord sends us into the world completely providing all the resources needed to fulfill this commission, the great Commission. Consider Paul's words in Ephesians:

Eph. 3:8 "The unsearchable (inexhaustible) riches of Christ."

As Eph. 3:20 would imply, "they are exceedingly abundant beyond anything we could ask, think or imagine:

So, the first of these Resources is:

21) <u>Love – A Perfectly Secure, eternally inseparable, unconditional love relationship</u>

Rom. 8:38,39 " For I am convinced that neither death, nor life, nor angels, nor principalities, nor things present, nor things to come, nor powers, nor height, nor depth, nor any other created thing, will be able to separate us from the love of God, which is in Christ Jesus our Lord."

A deep longing within the human heart is to love and to be loved. In our movies and other classic stories this theme is played out time and again, moving us within. And here is the ultimate love story of Jesus the true lover of our souls. It is He that has passionately sought us. He gave His life to rescue us from the Kingdom of Darkness to bring us into that intimate relationship. He will not lose a single one of us, His eternal bride. He longs for us to be with Him forever. We can give His love to others because we have experienced this unconditional love.

John 15:9 "Just as the Father has loved Me, I have also loved you; abide in My love."

1 John 4:19 "We love, because He first loved us"

Have you ever observed a guy who has just fallen in love? There is an air about him. The stars are brighter, the breeze is fresher, the beauty of the flowers and trees are more amazing. The world is simply a better place. You can be talking to him and his cell phone rings. It's his significant other, and he is gone. You have lost him.

Why is this? He feels special. What needs are being met by this relationship? His sense of self-worth is deeply enhanced. The one he highly esteems values him. That person brings out the best in him. She brings out in him a longing to be their better self. That love relationship resources him with strength, hope and motivation.

You and I were created for relationship. Remember, God created us in His image. He has eternally been in relationship Himself as Father, Son and Holy Spirit. The triune God has never been lonely, never been alone. From all eternity there has been a fellowship, a rich intimacy within the Trinity because the existence of persons within the Trinity is the source of the human personality. We know that God is personal for He has eternally been in a loving relationship: the Father with the Son and with the Spirit, the Son with the Spirit and the Father, and the Spirit with the Father and the Son. At the heart of all that is the heart of a person.

Again I remind us of what the philosopher Anselm put forward, "God is that being than which no greater being can exist." If God is not triune than prior to creation He was impersonal, without a person to love. Such a being would be lesser than one who is eternally relational. As three in one He has eternally been in a loving relationship.

Whatever it means to be human it innately means to be relational. Our greatest joys and pleasures come in our relationships. The parts of life that mean the most to us are family, friendships and falling in love. What are the greatest heartbreaks we experience? Would it not be when we lose a loved one? How do we punish people? We cut them off from us socially. We divorce them. In prison we put them in solitary confinement. We were made for relationships.

The quality, the significance, the depth of the person who loves us impacts us as well. The most significant other in the universe loves you unconditionally. You are perfectly secure in that inseparable love relationship. "We can love because He first loved us." 1John 4:19

This need for love has led many a person, and maybe you, to put up with being treated poorly by a person with whom they are in a relationship. Maybe you are single and you are dating someone who takes you for granted. You are allowing them to get away with things because you fear being alone. So you rationalize what more should I expect? Do you say to yourself, "I am damaged goods; I will never do better. I will live with this as long as they don't leave me."

Please evaluate if you are allowing someone to treat you in a way that Jesus never would. Dear Friend, that is looking for love in all the wrong places. We need to come into romantic relationships from positions of strength where the Lord Jesus has met our needs. His love allows us to face our brokenness. He can heal our wounds. His love is not judgmental, but He says, "Let me help you stop hurting yourself". Couples that are expecting to meet the deepest needs of one another are what Larry Crabbe calls "Two ticks looking for a dog". They will both be disappointed for only the Lord can meet their deepest needs. They need to look to Him to meet their needs and then love others as He has loved them.

In His strength we do have something that people are desperately looking for! I was at a conference of teachers in Russia recently. One of the teachers shared how difficult life was for many of the teachers she worked with. They were overwhelmed with their teaching load, their family responsibilities, the upkeep of their homes and their relationship with their spouses. So many of these teachers were weary of soul and were experiencing burn out. She went on to share, "We can deeply minister to people because what they need and the first thing we can give them is love. As we love them even those with hardness of heart will melt".

Love is the greatest privilege and power known to man. Love is a great resource that God has given His children that is available to us to impact our world. The first-century believers changed the course of history as they demonstrated a quality of love never before witnessed on this planet. The world around them marveled at how people from different cultures and stations in life like slaves and masters could be so bonded and so they marveled, "My how they love one another."

As we move out in faith The Lord will love people through us with His unconditional agape love. Psalm 139 expresses to us how God feels about each of His children.

Psalms 139:17, 18 "How precious also are Your thoughts to me, O God! How vast is the sum of them! If I should count them, they would outnumber the sand. When I awake, I am still with You."

You need to rest in His love. Let me ask, "Do you deep down believe He loves you?" He thinks about you all the time! You are on His heart every moment and never out of His thoughts. You are secure, desired, valued and special to Him. Jesus assures us of this love when He says in,

> John 17:23 "I in them and You in Me, that they may be perfected in unity, so that the world may know that You sent Me, and loved them, even as You have loved Me.."

Jesus experienced all the horrific torture of betrayal, beatings, scourging and death through crucifixion; one would be tempted to say to Jesus. "I thought You said the Father loved You? Jesus, do you call this love?" Jesus did not look at His suffering for proof of the Father's love, but He rested secure in the Father's love which strengthened Him to face the cross and endure its suffering and shame. This holds true for you and me, Believer. We are not to look at the circumstances in our lives asking the Lord to prove His love by giving us nice lives, delivering us from life's trials and complications. Hasn't He already proved His love?

> Rom. 5:8 "But God demonstrates His own love toward us, in that while we were yet sinners, Christ died for us."

We are able to face life and all it throws at us as we rest in His love and in its security. We are borne up through life's challenges. In the midst of those challenges we have His agape love to give even to the unlovable.

I think about my wife Jan all the time. When I am away from her I miss her and call her just to hear her wonderful voice. The safest place in the universe is standing in our kitchen with our arms around each other her head tucked under my chin. She is home for me. The security of her love and our marriage gives me the resources to handle all sorts of pressures. That is a picture for me of God's love.

Believer, you are perfectly secure in God's unconditional, eternally inseparable love. In the strength of that love we have much to give.

22) <u>New Creatures–A new creation, new man, new nature</u>

2 Cor. 5:17 "Therefore if anyone is in Christ, he is a new creature; the old things passed away; behold, new things have come."

What are those old things that have passed away? Attitudes have changed, habits have passed away, and desires are new and different. The way we talk and think has been revolutionized.

I am going to ask you to take a minute here to reflect on what God has done in your life. What has passed away in your life? Would you write down right now in the margin here three things that are old and have passed from your life?

For me it was my mouth. The Lord took away my foul speech and built into me words of encouragement. He took away my selfishness which led me to steal items at my place of work and replaced that selfishness with a heart to be a giver. He put in the past my desire to be a politician with power and prestige, and gave me in its place a heart for the lost of the world. So what about you? What has passed away and what has He made new? Take a little time and reflect on this.

There are areas in our lives that do not change immediately, but change on a more gradual basis as we grow. What is interesting is that because of inner change past desires no longer bring a sense of fulfillment to us. In fact, it is as if they do not belong to us or us to them.

One might say, "I was once a fish and my natural environment was water. I felt comfortable there. It was my nature that I belonged there. Now I am a cat. I am totally changed within. I am repelled by water. Throw me into water and I leap out. I don't fit. I don't belong there." My old pattern was parties and drinking and flirting with women. On becoming a Christian I still tried to fit into that old lifestyle, but my heart was changed, I was new. The old nature was no longer who I was.

73

Gal. 2:20 "I have been crucified with Christ ; and it is no longer I who live, but Christ lives in me; and the life which I now live in the flesh I live by faith in the Son of God, who loved me and gave Himself up for me."

That old scene didn't do it for me anymore. I felt out of place. I am so grateful the Lord took me out of that old life because I was heading in a downward spiral that was very harmful to me. It was a waste of my life. What is wonderful for you, Believer, is that God loves you so much He takes you just the way you are. And He loves you so much He is not going to leave you that way.

Think of how far you have come. Where would you be now without Jesus? What has the Lord surrounded your life with? How about the people He has placed in your life? My parents taught me to surround myself with people who lift me up, inspire me to be more as opposed to people who drag me or tear me down.

If you are in Christ, you have a new nature. You are a new creation. That changes who you are to the inner most part of you. You need to believe that what God says about you is true, the truest thing about you. What is key is thinking rightly or Biblically about yourself. There are issues in our lives that the Lord wishes to heal. We have deep wounds. People have deeply hurt us. You and I have believed lies about ourselves because of these wounds and hurts. You and I are new creations. The Lord wants to replace the lies that we have been telling or repeating to ourselves.

You might have deeply held beliefs such as "I really can't trust people or maybe not even the Lord." "I never do enough to make people happy with me." "I am not worthy of love". "It is not okay for me to need help". Are these true statements? No! A very real problem is that if you believe these lies they will affect you as if they were the truth. God wants to heal the wounds in my heart because that is where I am most vulnerable. The enemy's lies are usually based on and aimed at the wounds of my past. The longer I have believed these lies the deeper they go within me and they can become foundational to my belief system.

Ask the Lord where have you been wounded and what lies have you believed as a result of those wounds. We are new creatures. Old things have passed away, new things have come. You need to replace the lies of the past with the truth of God's Word.

You are brand new and you can say, "Others opinions of me or my performance should not determine my personal value. Only God has the right to tell me who I am." For example, here in Colossians is who you are.

Col. 2:9-10 "For in Him all the fullness of Deity dwells in bodily form, and in Him you have been <u>made complete,</u> and He is the head over all rule and authority;

I would like to share these ideas I learned from Maurice Wagner's, <u>Sensation of Being Somebody.</u>

"I am who I am because *I belong* to "the Father".

"I am who I am, *extremely valuable*, because "the Son" paid the ultimate price for me. The priceless blood of the lamb was shed for me."

"I am who I am because God the "Holy Spirit" lives in me and *makes me able and competent.*"

You have the resources to impact others' lives. You have a new mind with new perspectives. You get a fresh start every time you confess your sin and experience again God's love and forgiveness. Your heart of hearts, the new you, desires to please the Lord with your life.

There is the story of a captain of a ship in the British Royal Navy. He was a cruel and belligerent man. He demanded from the men on his ship extreme hours of labor. There was never allowed a moment of relief from his expectations. If he passed a crewman who even looked like he was not moving or was simply catching his breath the captain would unload on him cruel words and more severe work requirements. He belittled his crew, insulting them at every turn and created an environment of pure misery. He made Captain Bly appear to be a saint by comparison.

The Royal Navy of Britain became aware of this man and his method of leadership and flew a new captain by helicopter and dropped him down on the deck. The old captain was relieved of his command and put in the brig, the onboard jail.

The atmosphere aboard ship immediately changed. This new captain was a pleasure to be around. He led with praise and gratitude. The men took great pleasure being aboard ship and all they did seemed light and fun. Every now and then a crewman would pass close to the brig where the old captain was being held. The old captain would yell and say "What are you doing?" and give an order. The crewman would jump to attention and begin to perform as the old captain was ordering until he caught himself recognizing he was no longer under the authority of the old man. There was a new captain and the crewman owed his allegiance to him only.

I trust that you see the parallel here. You, Beloved, are freed from your old man. You are a new creation with a new Lord. The old nature has been circumcised off the real you. (Col. 2:10-12) You will hear the old nature which is still in this body of death express its desire and you will have a tendency to respond to the old nature's requests.

> Rom. 7:15-17 "For what I am doing, I do not understand; for I am not practicing what I would like to do, but I am doing the very thing I hate. But if I do the very thing I do not want to do, I agree with the Law, confessing that the Law is good. So now, no longer am I the one doing it, but sin which dwells in me."

But you do not have to listen to or obey your sin nature. You have a new heart and you are a new creation. In the resources of being a new creation your new desires will bring glory to God. New things have come to you, which the Lord has made true to enable you to step out in faith to bring Him Glory.

23) <u>You received the greatest Goal—"Becoming like Christ"</u>

> Rom. 8:29 "For those whom He foreknew, He also predestined to become conformed to the image of His Son, so that He would be the firstborn among many brethren;"

Col. 3:10 "and have put on the new self who is being renewed to a true knowledge according to the image of the One who created him"

Here is another resource we take into the spiritual battle for winning the lost to Christ and accomplishing God's eternal purposes in our lives. The Lord's goal for our lives is to make us like His Son. This helps my perspective as well as giving me an advantage of expressing the character of the Lord in my daily dealing with people. In eternity, I will have a resurrected body like Jesus' but I will also have a perfect moral character like His. I will no longer have an inner attraction and actually sin won't ever cross my mind. Then it will be complete and totally evident. Today it is mine as I walk by faith and the Lord transforms me day by day to be more like Jesus. Notice this does not come by self- effort.

Phil. 1:6 "For I am confident of this very thing, that He who began a good work in you will perfect it until the day of Christ Jesus".

It is the Lord who began the good work in you. He initiated the work and the work will not be complete until you go home to be with the Lord or the Lord returns for you.

Jan and I had the privilege to meet Dr. Bill Bright and his wife Vonette one evening in their home. We were invited to meet with them along with about forty other new staff. We were told their home was right near the old hotel where we were staying but we could not find it and showed up at their front door ten minutes late. We had to knock on the door with Dr. Bright standing in front of the door as he was addressing everyone who had already arrived. We timidly knocked on that door and Dr. Bright answered. Jan spoke up and said, "Dr. Bright, we got lost". His warm reply was, "That's all right Dear. We all like sheep have gone astray. Come on in." Wide eyed, we entered, sat and listened to his heart as he shared his vision for the world and our call as a movement. His warmth and love for the Savior drew us in. He engaged us with vision for the world. As we walked away from that time together and back to our room in the hotel I remember saying to Jan, "Honey I don't know why, but I love that guy." And then it hit me! I knew why I loved him. I love Him because I saw my Savior in Him. I clearly saw Jesus in his life. How could I help but love him?

There is something about the person of Jesus that has been a motivation in my life. It especially helps me as I relate to men evangelistically. There are so many ways men try to impress each other. In some cultures this concept is called machismo, in others it's macho. In America there are phrases like "You da man". Men are very socially conscience of coming across in a way that other men respect. When I look at Jesus, I see a man who is completely secure. He is the perfectly masculine man. Men express their masculinity in so many false ways. In the weight room it is how much you can lift and how defined you are physically. At the party it is how much you can drink, how well you hold your liquor, how crazy you are and how many people you can entertain. I've known men who were addicted to laughter and would do anything as long as someone would laugh. Some guys want to demonstrate how many other men they can make feel inferior through their quick and cutting wit. A man truly is not measured by how wealthy he is or by the impressiveness of the things he possesses.

I would argue that Jesus is the perfect model of a man. He was a man of uncompromising principles, unswerving convictions and an unmarred character. There was a tremendous strength about Him and yet the ability to be tender and compassionate. A real man is not one who takes, but rather gives. Does he build people up or tear them down? Does a woman feel better about herself or worse after spending time with him? Is there graciousness about him like that evidenced in Jesus' life? As a man one can stand identified with Jesus in any male arena. In Jesus we have the ultimate man's man.

One of the biggest thrills for me is that I have been able to raise my son around quality male college students and other godly men. These men have hung out with him, loved him and included him into their activities. On the summer leadership project we led for eighteen years we had a number of emphases directed toward the male heart, one of which was a men's conference. This was not a time for sitting around sharing precious verses. Rather, it was a very physically demanding time that would lead to the men rallying to look out for each other, carrying each other, admonishing each other and deeply sharing their hearts with one another.

My son, from the age of eleven, was included in on these times. The images of true masculinity were imprinted on him. He made friends with young men who became his heroes. Years later he became a student on the project himself when he entered college. To this day he has a special heart to be a man's man and to reach men in all sorts of male environments for the Savior. He seems to be able to create the climate where men feel drawn, where they feel believed in and where they can be real with one another.

I imagine it is a little hard to relate to this if you are a woman, though you would not mind seeing more men with the character of Jesus. Take to heart that you can relate better to being the bride of Christ than we can as men. The instant you and I became believers it became the Lord's goal to conform us to the image of Christ.

In this Song by Evie Turnquist Karlsson, she expresses a heart for becoming like Christ. The verse that follows shows the Biblical principle behind the concept of Christ-likeness and how God is transforming us.

Mirror, Mirror on the wall, I know who is Lord of all

Just let me see Him every day

To me that is the only way

2 Cor. 3:17, 18 "Now the Lord is the Spirit, and where the Spirit of the Lord is, there is freedom. And we, who with unveiled faces all reflect the Lord's glory, are being transformed into His likeness with ever-increasing glory, which comes from the Lord, who is the Spirit." (NIV)

We have this divine calling and this resource of Christ likeness. Are you progressing to becoming more and more like Him every day? That Christ-like quality, that good work that the Lord has begun is a tremendously attractive quality in a believer. We have this resource working in us as we move out in faith to reach those who do not know Christ.

24) <u>The Power of Christ's Resurrection</u>

> Eph.1:18-20 " I pray that the eyes of your heart may be enlightened, so that you will know what is the hope of His calling, what are the riches of the glory of His inheritance in the saints, and what is the surpassing greatness of His power toward us who believe. These are in accordance with the working of the strength of His might which He brought about in Christ, when He raised Him from the dead and seated Him at His right hand in the heavenly places,"

This power is ours to draw on. Paul's prayer is that you and I would have the spiritual discernment to know and live in the truth that we have the surpassing greatness of His power. It is a power that is according to the very power of Almighty God Himself. This is the very power that conquered death in the resurrection of Christ.

Let's consider this question. What did Christ's resurrection destroy? Death, Sin and Satan

> Death is humanity's worst fear.
> Sin is our hearts most daunting problem.
> Satan is our number one enemy.

Let's examine how Christ's resurrection defeats these three great enemies. If death which is humanity's worst fear, has been defeated then consider this. The many other fears we experience are defeated as well. Think about these various things of which people are afraid: failure, embarrassment, public speaking, injury, rejection, loneliness, darkness, pain, abuse, punishment, suffering, crowds and a financial crisis.

<u>Fears:</u> In our position in Christ we have the resources to face these and overcome our fears. Since the resurrection is the defeat of our worst fear, death, we are able to confront our personal fears. How

do I confront these in the power of the resurrection? Well how has the resurrection overcome the fear of death? Paul says in Philippians, "To live is Christ, to die is gain." I can personally face that fear by recognizing I have nothing that can ultimately harm me, actually it improves my situation. When believers die, they go to heaven. Jesus even encouraged, "Do not fear those who can merely kill the body but are unable to harm the soul, but rather fear Him who is able to destroy both body and soul in hell." Matt. 10:28

I can face rejection because Christ's resurrection has yielded ultimate acceptance from the most significant other in the universe as well as the love of other believers. I can face each of these fears and more because if God is for me who can be against me. And if someone is who cares.

Truly fear could be something utterly overwhelming for you. If so, there is far deeper advice that you may gain from a discipler or counselor. The point to be made here is that you do have the positional resources to overcome. As a result of overcoming your fear, your faith will grow, you will grow as a person, and the possibilities will expand for seeing the Lord use you and expand the possibilities that are presented in your life. Stepping out in faith is risk taking, and it is likely stepping out of your comfort zone.

I have had the opportunity to take a group of believers into some intimidating environments to speak about a relationship with Christ. As we have gathered together to brief ourselves on speaking to a group, I felt my heart pound and have looked into people's eyes and seen a good bit of nervousness and in some situations downright fear. As we would pray in preparation we would remind ourselves of who we are in Christ. We are sons and daughters of the King. We are totally accepted in the Beloved. We are able to love because He first loved us. Therefore thus prepared we go in the power of His resurrection.

We would go to the meeting house or the room where the group met or lived and by faith we would share the good news of Jesus. As teammates we have shared before highly successful athletic teams, fraternities, gatherings of elite scientists, conferences of educators, city councils, meetings of influential business men and women, government officials and many different collections of university students. Time and again we have seen the Lord give us favor and have been well received by these various groups and time and again we have seen great response to the message of Christ. Even our worse fears are not going to end up costing as much as we have feared they might.

My wife Jan was invited to speak to an African American Sorority. At that time in her life she was wrestling with anxiety and speaking was very difficult for her. The opportunity was so wonderful she agreed to speak. In the middle of her presentation her nervousness got the better of her as her worst fears actually occurred. She had a bit of a panic attack and could hardly breathe. The women in the sorority were so kind and gracious. They had her sit down. They encouraged her that it was okay and that they would wait until she could finish. She caught her breath finished her talk and half a dozen women trusted Jesus for the first time and met weekly for follow-up over that last semester. The Lord overcame her fear by letting that which she most feared occur and doing great things in spite of it.

Phil. 4:13 I can do all things through Him who strengthens me.

Our sin problem: Is there a sin defeating you? Maybe it is an habitual sin? It has been harming your walk with God far too long.

Some of the sin we face is a simple matter of being convicted as we hit the conviction point, confessing it, turning from it and moving on. I would call that "*comma confession*".

Then there is falling into sin by ignoring or rebelling at the conviction point. That necessitates our pausing and reflecting on how we yielded to a temptation and steps we need to take to yield to the Lord and be filled with the Spirit again. That would be "*semi-colon*" confession.

If a sin has a greater hold on you than the above descriptions it is time to agree with God that you do not hate that sin. He does, but you do not. It is time to do prescription Bible study. This is "*period confession*". Ask the Lord to give you His heart and to be able to see that sin as He sees it.

Gal. 5:24-25 "Now those who belong to Christ Jesus have crucified the flesh with its passions and desires. If we live by the Spirit, let us also walk by the Spirit."

You belong to Jesus. Since that is true what follows is in the past tense. You have crucified the flesh. Christian, it is past tense, it is executed and dead. You are not alive to the flesh.

If you are wrestling with sin even though you long for victory let me give you two suggestions. *One* has to do with the put-offs and put-ons as explained by Paul in Ephesians four. This is part of the *period* confession.

> Eph. 4:22-30 "You were taught, with regard to your former way of life, to put off your old self, which is being corrupted by its deceitful desires; to be made new in the attitude of your minds; and to put on the new self, created to be like God in true righteousness and holiness. Therefore each of you must put off falsehood and speak truthfully to his neighbor, for we are all members of one body. "In your anger do not sin": Do not let the sun go down while you are still angry, and do not give the devil a foothold. He who has been stealing must steal no longer, but must work, doing something useful with his own hands, that he may have something to share with those in need. Do not let any unwholesome talk come out of your mouths, but only what is helpful for building others up according to their needs, that it may benefit those who listen. "(NIV)

You will notice in this passage that for every put off there is a put on. We are to put off the old nature activity not only by stopping this sin but instead stepping into the new man activity. As you choose this the Spirit empowers you and renews your heart. You are a new creation. Instead of taking as a thief, you give away what you have earned with your own hands. You are not lying, but you are speaking the truth. You don't speak unkindly or utter words that are profane, rather the words you speak uplift and encourage the hearts of those around you. This is a total change of heart which you possess because you are this new spiritual person. A another example is found in Phil. 4:6, 7

> "Be anxious for nothing, but in everything by prayer and sup-
> plication with thanksgiving let your requests be made known

to God. And the peace of God, which surpasses all comprehension, will guard your hearts and your minds in Christ Jesus."

You and I are commanded not to be anxious. Our old nature is guilty of this. But if you step into the new nature activities you are empowered by the Holy Spirit to do what is true of the new you. You, in your heart of hearts, are drawn to trust the Lord in prayer. What is the promise if you will do as Paul instructs? Peace, which will guard your heart and mind. What kind of peace? This is a peace which is beyond comprehension and which is the opposite of anxiety.

For every sin that we might struggle with, there is a new nature activity to replace it. That is my first suggestion. If you are struggling with an habitual sin you need to do a prescription Bible study and ask the Lord to give you the *"put-on"* in His Word for the sin you struggle with.

The final suggestion comes from Neal Anderson's book <u>Bondage Breaker</u>. This is what I would refer to as *"exclamation point confession"*. This last form of confession is necessary when the evil one has gotten a stronghold in a person's life. A believer needs to break the bondage. I have made use of this process of taking back turf I have surrendered and have found these steps so freeing and refreshing. Make use of this *"exclamation point"* confession. In his book Neal shares a step by step process one needs to take to reclaim territory that has been yielded to the enemy of our souls. If you are struggling with an habitual sin, very likely you have given the enemy a foothold. He explains how to gain back this territory by confronting the deception the evil one led you to believe.

My suggestion to you is if his thoughts strike a chord with you, please get his book and learn directly from him.

No enemy, no fear and no problem can defeat you. That is power! It is power that is ours when we step out in faith and appropriate it. This is power of His resurrection.

<u>Enemies of our faith:</u> The Church faces many who wish to oppose it and the progress of the gospel. God's people are going to face opposition from the devil. He is opposed to everything believers stand for and he hates anyone who is sold out to Jesus Christ. He will

do anything he can to defeat you. Believers are hated because Satan and those of the world's system hate Jesus. Anyone who is trying to do something for God will face some opposition.

John 15:18-22 "If the world hates you, keep in mind that it hated me first. If you belonged to the world, it would love you as its own. As it is, you do not belong to the world, but I have chosen you out of the world. That is why the world hates you. Remember the words I spoke to you: 'No servant is greater than his master.' If they persecuted me, they will persecute you also. If they obeyed my teaching, they will obey yours also. They will treat you this way because of my name, for they do not know the One who sent me. (NIV)

All believers who seek to live godly lives face opposition at some time in their lives.

There are many Christians today who live in countries where they are persecuted for their faith. In many circumstances it is "Reject Jesus or lose your job or be kicked out of the family" or worse. Paul serves as the example of one who saw ultimate victory over enemies of the faith.

He lived a very powerful life. He was responsible for writing most of the New Testament. He took the news of Jesus Christ into the world with a passion and attitude more befitting a soldier than a pastor! You couldn't keep this guy down! You could beat him, flog him, throw him in stocks, imprison him, humiliate him, and spit on him. You could take him within an inch of his life, and he would still be talking about Jesus.

Paul's power sure didn't come from his physical prowess. He was frail and possibly nearsighted. Paul himself speaks of his own frail body a few times in his letters. He set up church after church in city after city, as hundreds of thousands gave their lives to Christ. For Paul, though that involved being constantly afflicted, he had a great perspective through it all.

2 Cor. 4:17,18 "For momentary, light affliction is producing for us an eternal weight of glory far beyond all comparison,

while we look not at the things which are seen, but at the things which are not seen; for the things which are seen are temporal, but the things which are not seen are eternal."

Now what about your situation, with your non-Christian friends, or family, colleagues and neighbors? Don't you often find that there is a subtle pressure for you to shut up about Jesus? What do we do when we face opposition? How does your position in Christ and the power of Christ's resurrection defeat this enemy?

Before the Lord in prayer, even out loud, claim your position and then let the enemy know he has no right, no claim. Remind the evil one that you are the Lord's; this battle is the Lord's.

2 Cor. 10:3-5 "For though we live in the world, we do not wage war as the world does. The weapons we fight with are not the weapons of the world. On the contrary, they have divine power to demolish strongholds. We demolish arguments and every pretension that sets itself up against the knowledge of God, and we take captive every thought to make it obedient to Christ." (NIV)

Pray for the removal of the obstacle to the furtherance of the Gospel. I believe we are able to say, "Move out of the way!"

Matt. 17:20 "And He said to them, "Because of the littleness of your faith; for truly I say to you, if you have faith the size of a mustard seed, you will say to this mountain, 'Move from here to there,' and it will move ; and nothing will be impossible to you."

We have very little need to move actual mountains but there are major barriers we face that need to be moved out of the way so that the Kingdom can move forward. I have seen many an authority try to block the progress of the gospel and folks prayed, saying, "Lord change that person or remove him or her from their position." The Lord has changed the heart or removed coaches, heads of student housing, presidents of colleges, educational administrators and governmental leaders. Believer, your position in Christ is one of power!

Recall what happened when Jesus healed the paralytic whose friends lowered him through the roof in front of Him. He addressed the man and said to him, "Rise take up your pallet, walk and go home." The man took Jesus at His word. He immediately rose up picked up that pallet and left the room. He did not sit up half way and think, "Wow, this is nice. Wow, I have never done that before. I might hang out here for a while." No. He believed what Jesus said and was empowered to do as Jesus commanded. In eternity we will be visibly and undeniably powerful. Then it will be by sight. Now it is by faith. This is the case with all our positional truths. In heaven we will have as perfect a righteousness as Jesus. Today God has declared that as true, but we have to take it by faith. Then it will be by sight. So, Believer, you have available to you the power of Christ's resurrection. You are powerful. Take it by faith and step out in faith to see victory in these three areas.

We are able to face the various fears that surface in our lives and see the Lord give us the confidence we need and special results He provides. We have the power to live holy lives and see victory over struggle or sin. We are able to stand victorious before enemies and confront the opposition that would oppose our Lord, "For He who is in us is greater than He who is in the world." (1Jn. 4:4) Perhaps there is some leader standing in the way preventing the progress of the gospel. Approach that leader with the courtesy that Daniel showed when he asked to be tested for ten days regarding his diet. He did not put his overseer at risk for his life or his job. Ask only for what is needed in such a wise and gracious manner. Then pray about it and watch the Lord move the barriers or remove the key person.

25) <u>Promises to supply all my needs</u>

Phil. 4:19 "And my God will supply all your needs according to His riches in glory in Christ Jesus."

Notice here what God is saying as well as what He is not saying. This is supplying our needs not our wants. Living in our position in

Christ is not "name it claim it". Paul is grateful for the loving concern of the Philippian church. He is rejoicing with the Philippians because they have ministered to him by sending a gift through Epaphroditus as he visited Paul in prison in Rome. The Philippians had given to Paul sacrificially and Paul was confident that the Lord would supply for the Philippians in their need. The Philippians had no reason to worry because the Lord would meet their needs not just out of His riches, but according to those riches.

I was sharing this series on positional truth at a fall retreat with students from Bowling Green State University. I got a phone call from my wife, Jan, She said, "Honey I have some pretty bad news about Chelle's upcoming surgery". Our daughter was born with a congenital heart defect and was going to have a very expensive open heart surgery in a few months. Because she is adopted the insurance company said they would not cover her surgery and Jan and I would be left being responsible for an operation that was going to cost over $40,000. This was overwhelming to us on two counts. One it seemed to reduce our daughter to less than a recognized member of our family. The second strain was financial. Everything seemed to be at risk. We had no clue how to come up with such a sum.

"Well, Jim," the question the Lord put in my thoughts, "do you really believe the stuff you are teaching?" I shared with Jan over the phone, "I don't know how, Honey, but the Lord is going to make this operation possible and somehow it will get paid for." There is nothing that can come into our lives to ruin them. Every circumstance and situation has to go through the Lord. He has promised to meet all our needs whether physical, mental, spiritual or material.

We are part of a movement that is pro-life and who regard adoption as a very positive way to form a family. They went to bat with our insurance company and they reversed their decision. Three months later we got this news. Even the $3,000 that remained after the deductibles that we needed to pay was graciously met by our support team. Chelle's operation was a wonderful success. We have seen time and again the Lord provide for the needs of our Chelle who has special needs. He has provided Special Olympics for her to make friends and to enjoy success.

The Lord meets needs in our lives other than material or financial. He met a need in our family that deeply touched our son's personal development and well-being. My son, Dan, went to a large high school that was very academically and socially competitive, and he did not thrive in that environment. There were some students in his youth group from a different school with whom he connected really well. This school was smaller and had a more relaxed feel. Jan found out that this high school had open enrollment and applied to have Dan accepted. Dan's heart leapt at the possibility and his hopes soared. We knew that the likelihood of his being accepted were very slim. I recall a family time when Jan, not wanting him to be crushed, cautioned that this might not come to pass. Having embraced these positional truths I felt led to claim one. "Lord, Dan needs this school. He needs this smaller environment." "Dan", I said, "the Lord is going to make this happen. We are going to claim this aspect of the Lord's nature. He knows your need and knowing the character of the Lord, He is not going to give you a scorpion instead of a fish. He will provide for you through this school." Four months later we got the letter. He was one of only two students accepted for their open enrollment. As it turned out it was the last year the school board was allowed to have open enrollment. That school, its great environment and the opportunities he had there as well as his many friends, made the greatest difference in his life. He came into his own and flourished.

The Lord promises to supply your needs.

26) Joint Heirs with Christ
You are filthy stinking rich.

Rom. 8:17a "and if children, heirs also, heirs of God and fellow-heirs with Christ,"

What does it mean to be a joint-heir? It means that everything that Jesus is an heir to is available to us as well. So what is Christ an heir to? He is heir to the throne. He will rule as King over all the earth. He is reigning presently in heaven. He is King of kings and Lord of lords. As creator of all things (Col. 1:16, 17), all things are headed to a climatic end in Him for Him and through Him. He owns it all. He lacks nothing. He is rich beyond comprehension. You are a joint heir with Him. Do you see how wealthy you are? This is what is available to you.

Our Chelle, loves crafts of all kinds. She is quite the collector of various different interests as they strike her. She has made hundreds of string friendship bracelets. Thus she has these clear plastic boxes with dozens of compartments filled with a tremendous variety of different colors of string. She likes to make necklaces and bracelets of beads and has boxes and boxes of all types of shapes, sizes and colors of beads. She crochets and as you can imagine she has numerous finished blankets and owns barrels of yarn. She has bookcases filled with lots of animated movies and dozens of PG movies. She has other bookcases loaded down with Christian romance novels. You would be amazed at how many have been written.

Now Michelle is my heir but sometimes she has drawn on her inheritance inappropriately. You see for a while Chelle was stealing money from her mom and me. She would take the money and buy these items of interest to her. She was breaking our hearts in two ways when she would do this. One, it was so agonizing that she was actually stealing. Her rational was that she wanted something and had no money. It was crushing to realize that was her attitude. The second thing she was stealing from us was the opportunity to meet her heart's desire as a gift from us. There is little that is as special or just plain fun as taking her to the store and watching her eyes light up and her heart fill with glee as we, together, pick out one of those special items for her. So Friend let me ask you if you are giving the Lord opportunity to let you draw on your inheritance?

Matt. 7: 7 11 "And I say to you, ask and shall be given unto you: seek and you shall find; knock and it shall be opened to you; for everyone who asks, receives; and he who seeks, finds and to him who knocks, it shall be opened. Now suppose one of you fathers is asked by his son for a fish; he will not give him a snake instead of a fish, will he? Or if he is asked for an egg, he will not give him a scorpion; will he, or a loaf of bread will give him a stone? If you then. Being evil, know how to give good gifts to your children, how much more shall your heavenly Father give what is good to those who ask Him?"

For a number of years I had the privilege of leading a summer leadership project of over a hundred university students on the coast of New Jersey. I was responsible for finding housing for the students and staff. We would rent a large beach house that would get closed for the winter and opened back up each summer. Many times the landlord would be unreasonable about price or needed improvements. I even had one landlord that felt because we were Christians, we would put up with anything, so he sought to exploit that.

We turned to the Lord and prayed, "Oh Lord, we believe these summers are so beneficial for the furtherance of the kingdom that we would ask to draw on our inheritance. Would you provide us housing that would allow us to avoid dealing with these difficult landlords and provide housing ideally conducive for developing these students as leaders? For Your glory and for the furtherance of the kingdom please provide this".

Well, the Lord did that in wonderful abundance. A great friend of ours who lived at the shore, called me saying, "Jim there is a place down here I think would be ideal. The building is shut down and the owner is being foreclosed on, I think if you could get a partnership of buyers you could get it at a good price," The Lord raised up four men who went together and bought the place at a price well below market value. They also gave us the great blessing of letting us do anything to the house that would make it ideal for our purposes. Jehovah Jireh!

In the movie "Battle of the Bulge" I believe there is an excellent picture of what it looks like to be richly supplied in the battle. By late 1944, Germany was at a real crucial point in the war they were losing. The Soviet Red Army was closing in on the Eastern front. The Italian peninsula had been captured and liberated, and the Allied armies were advancing rapidly through France toward Germany and Berlin.

The battle was fought on an eighty mile front running from southern Belgium through the Ardennes Forest, and over to Ettelbruck in the middle of Luxembourg. Hitler's real target was the British-American alliance, and he saw the battle as a juggernaut to break apart and defeat the Allied forces. That "surprise attack" would supposedly divide British and American forces, leaving the way wide open for the German army to swing north and seize the port of Antwerp. Thus they could cut off the main supply base for the Allied armies on the Western Front. Hitler felt he had to turn the momentum.

However there was a problem. A critically important need for the German army was fuel. This was highlighted by a scene in the movie. The German Colonel responsible for the German tank division met in his General's office. He had in his possession a box. He set the box in front of the general and said, "This is the reason the Americans are going to win the war!" The general opened the box and remarked, "This is a chocolate cake. What does this have to do with winning the war?" "Taste it!" the colonel said. "It is rather good." the general replied. "Yes, and notice how fresh it is. Would you like to know where we acquired the cake? It was with some American troops we captured on the front line. The Americans have no sense of losing! We are not confident we can get all our equipment into the battle much less back from it. The Americans have so much fuel they are able to send chocolate cake to the front lines, 'Fresh chocolate cake!' We must move immediately. We must win this battle and break their will or the war will be lost for good!" the colonel emphatically stated.

The Battle of the Bulge began with a German attack on the morning of December 16, 1944. Under cover of heavy fog, thirty-eight German divisions struck along a fifty mile front. On December 23, American forces began their first counterattack on the southern flank of the "bulge." Losses on both sides were terribly high. The Germans were being bled dry of fuel and resources. On January 7, 1945, Hitler agreed with his staff to pull back most of his forces from the Ardennes, thus ending all offensive operations. On January 8, German troops withdrew from the tip of the "bulge." Their losses were critical. The last of the German reserves were gone, the Luftwaffe had been broken, and the German army in the west was being pushed back. With the majority of its air power and men lost, Germany had few forces left to defend the Third Reich. Germany's final defeat loomed just a few months away. At the end of the movie you see German soldiers utterly abandoning thousands of pieces of their weapons, equipment and empty tanks in the field and walking back to Germany having lost the "Battle of the Bulge".

You and I are facing spiritual battles every day. Sometimes we are advancing into the enemy's territory seeking to rescue the perishing. Sometimes the battle is more on the home front facing challenges in our personal lives. Opportunities may be given to us that require stepping out in faith to see the Lord glorified, but it also often requires a resource we seem to lack. Well Dear Friend, the supply lines are open and our Lord and commander in chief will see to it that we have the resource we need to come out victorious for His glory. What are you facing?

What we have talked about in this section is that resources are yours as you step out in faith for the Lord. As you do, what kinds of barriers do you encounter? Are finances needed to make it possible for you to get training to enable you to lead something for the Lord? Is it a facility needed for the work of the ministry? How about tuition for schooling for preparation to serve? You want to go to the mission field, but there seem to be so many obstacles in the way. Specifically share each of them with the Lord. You are a joint-heir with Christ. You need to know that the Lord has set up a trust fund for His heirs. We trust and He funds.

> James 4:2, 3 "You have not because you ask not." You ask
> and do not receive, because you ask with wrong motives, so
> that you may spend it on your pleasures.

We need to recognize we are in real spiritual battle with great opportunities to advance the Lord's cause, bringing Him glory. We are to step out in faith trusting Him to supply the resources necessary to accomplish His will, drawing on that "trust fund". And Dear Friend it just so happens that many times He will send along with the resource some chocolate cake.

POSITIONAL TRUTH SERIES
CHAPTER # 5

Rights and Promises of the Believer

The Christian life is meant to be a power-packed life with sustained victory over sin. It is to involve delightful intimacy with the Lord and wonderful impact for His kingdom. We have looked at how the Lord has provided for our *relationship* with Him. He has made us *righteous* in Christ. He has given us the Holy Spirit (The *Restrainer*) the one who comes with strength to aid us in our walk and witness. He has given us the *resources* so that we can see His purposes fulfilled. Next we are going to look at the *rights and promises* that are ours as we go up against the enemy of our faith in the authority of Christ.

This next part of positional truth involves a little more understanding of the *epic* and the great conflicts of science fiction like "Star Wars". I love the imagination of these works and how they picture and illustrate rich truths. There are vivid pictures in stories like Terry Brooks' "Shannara" series, C.S. Lewis' "Chronicles of Narnia" and Tolkien's "Lord of the Rings". These stories bring to life concrete truths. They are allegories, truth in story form. One truth that comes through in Tolkien's "Lord of the Rings" is the revelation that the further Frodo and Sam Wise get to their goal, Mordor, the dwelling place of Sauron, the closer they get to the heart of the enemy. That leads to greater struggle, burden and resistance. The weight of the task seems overwhelming. What a parallel to what we face as the church. As the gospel advances and penetrates more and more into strongholds of the enemy we don't simply face challenges or obstacles, we face the enemy, and his minions. Since this is the case, we need to exercise our authority as believers claiming our rights and promises.

In the same way as Frodo advances in "The Lord of the Rings" I would have us consider that the more advances we see of our Lord's gospel and growth of the kingdom, the closer we will come to the heart of the enemy, and we will see increasingly more resistance from him. Spiritual warfare becomes a greater and greater issue and living out our position in Christ becomes vitally necessary.

Conversion of people is not taking them and putting them in an armchair so they glide easily to heaven. It is the beginning of a mighty conflict which costs us much to win the victory. This battle, or better the war, is as real and true as any war the world has known. Far too many Christians live as if they are living in a recreation room rather than on a battlefield. Yet this war is of far greater importance than any war that has ever been fought.

True Christianity is a fight. The Scriptures tell us we are soldiers. The Christian is to be a "Man of War". Our principle fight is with the world, the flesh and the devil, our chief enemies. Victory must be won here. There is the exertion of spiritual warfare which means battling to say "no", when the world, the flesh and the devil urge you to say "yes" and saying "yes", when weariness, deadness and unbelief prompt you to say "no".

The Christian fight is a good fight because it is fought with the best of means for eternal results. We fight with all the rights and promises of God. We stand in His armor. We have wonderful promises of victory from a living God who cannot lie. He has granted us the authority as believers to claim these rights and promises. There is no doubt that it is a war in which there is tremendous struggle and agony and there will be conflict with bruises and wounds. There needs to be discipline, focus and great exertion. Here is God's promise in Rom. 8:37 to every believer without exception "But in all these things we overwhelmingly conquer through Him who loves us." In this company to which all believers are called, there is to be no one missing in action!

It can be hard for us to feel we are worthy or able to live in this authority that is ours as believers. So often we feel we have disappointed in simple points of trust. "Oh Lord, I have failed You again! How am I to draw on these rights in what seems to be an even more challenging situation?" Let us remember that not one of us could win if left to our own strength or if we relied on our own ability. It is His promise and His Word that prevails.

The promises of God are certain to be kept. He is almighty. Nothing can prevent His doing what He has said. He never changes. He is always "of one mind" (Job 23:13) and with Him "there is no variation or shadow of turning."(James 1:17) He will always keep His Word. We need Him. He is the one under whose wings we abide and in the midst of the turmoil when the battle gets fierce it is most helpful to remember that He is our fortress and He is our shelter.

Every great story has simply borrowed from the greatest of adventures and romances of the story of salvation. Our great hero, Jesus, has shown His precious love for his future bride. Jesus has faced the most heinous and wicked of enemies. In great stories there are extraordinary challenges and many sacrifices to be made for that which is most honorable, extremely noble and for a cause which surpasses oneself. For example, in Lewis' novels the sacrifice is for the love of the Lord. In Tolkien's "Lord of the Rings", we see the bonds of brotherhood and a fellowship where sacrifice is about being part of an heroic story.

We are at war. We also are in a love story. This is set in the midst of a life and death battle. We have reached the moment where we, too, must find our courage and rise up to rescue and fight for the hearts of others. Jesus calls us to be His intimate ally, to recognize that as His sons and daughters we can be involved and victorious in the great battle for the hearts of those we love and for those of the men and women of the world.

Now for those positional truths that enable us to face the enemy, we will consider Our *rights* and p*romises*. We are going to examine the next nine positional truths that become ours the instant we put our trust in Christ and become Christians. Please be patient because this concept is a lot more difficult for me to explain.

27) <u>Citizens of Heaven</u>

Phil. 3:20 "For our citizenship is in heaven, from which also we eagerly wait for a Savior, the Lord Jesus Christ;"

There is a great deal of difference between the status of a slave and that of a citizen. Citizens have privileges as an insider and they have the freedom to take advantage of all opportunities. A slave may get food and shelter but, he has nothing he can call his own, not his time, not himself and not his choices. *You* are a citizen.

If you were on a trip in a foreign country and found yourself in legal difficulty, do you know where you might go for help? As a citizen of your home nation you could appeal to your nation's embassy. There you would have reason to believe they would come to your aid, or at least represent your legal rights.

If I had problems I would go to the American Embassy. As a citizen of the United States I have rights so I could expect them to protect me and defend me. We call these our "inalienable rights". There are a number of times throughout the book of Acts that Paul is seen exercising his Roman citizenship. He did this in response to the government authorities of his day.

We face the ruler of this age, the prince of the power of the air. According to the Scriptures you are not a slave to sin or the law but a citizen of heaven. Why would the Lord want us to know this? What does this entitle us to? Certainly when we have trouble here and find ourselves facing the enemy, it is crucial we realize our heavenly citizenship. We don't want to face the enemy's minions without the Lord's engagement. Have you ever exercised your rights as a citizen of heaven? My hope is that you will learn in this chapter about those rights and feel equipped to draw on these positional truths.

We are on foreign turf. We are behind enemy lines, aren't we? We are aliens, strangers, pilgrims and sojourners.

1 Peter 2:11 "Beloved, I urge you as aliens and strangers to abstain from fleshly lusts which wage war against the soul."

This world is not our home. When we became believers the Lord changed our status. This is a status where we are not at home in this world, and are now no longer outsiders with the Lord.

Ephesians 2:19 *"So then you are no longer strangers and aliens, but you are fellow citizens with the saints, and are of God's household,"*

I would argue that men and women of faith throughout Biblical history have recognized this world as the current possession of the evil one and saw the need to invade enemy territory. In this time of history we need some Daniels, Josephs, Pauls and Tituses, who are citizens with authority, who recognize that we have promised victories, citizens who know how to exercise their rights and promises.

Look at Jesus' perspective on this from Matt. 16:18

"Upon this rock I will build My church; and the gates of Hell will not overpower it".

According to Jesus who is on the attack? I believe it is we, the Church, God's people. I think we commonly view this as if we are the ones hiding behind gates, and at times lowering the draw bridge and opening the gates, we send a few of our own to seek out and rescue a few of the perishing. We find a few, bring them back to the fortress, raise the draw bridge, close the gates, panting in safety as we catch our breath and celebrate our winnings. No, My Friend, we are not the ones behind gates. It is we who go to Satan's citadel, his turf, and pound on his gates and they do not prevail against us! We pound on his gates by advancing into strongholds where he holds sway, by sharing the gospel with the lost or by tearing down belief systems that are contrary to God's truth.

Let's look at some Biblical examples because we need to realize that like these men and women we are promised victories all throughout Scripture. Israel received promises of victory from the Lord. Consider the promise made to Moses at his calling at the burning bush.

Ex 3:8 "So I have come down5 to rescue them from the hand of the Egyptians and to bring them up out of that land into a good and spacious land, a land flowing with milk and honey." (NIV)

How did Israel do with this promise of taking possession of the Promised Land? They sent out the twelve spies out one from each of the tribes as Numbers 13:1-14:19 describes. These twelve went into Canaan and came back forty days later with a majority report and a minority report. They discovered that the land was an extremely fruitful place just as the Lord promised. It did indeed flow with milk and honey. But the majority, ten of the spies, said, "We cannot possibly think of taking it because it has fortified cities and there are giants living there and we are like grasshoppers in their sight." Caleb and Joshua, in the minority, encouraged, "We should by all means go up and take possession of it, for we shall surely overcome it."

Well, Israel cowered in unbelief. They not only refused to obey the Lord to go in and take the land, they voiced desire to stone Joshua and Caleb. What a contrast to how David responded upon seeing the giant, Goliath, taunt the armies of the living God. The Israeli army saw giants and they thought that they were so big they could not possibly hit them. David saw a giant and believed the giant was so big he couldn't possibly miss him! He attacked, the giant fell, and the Philistines were routed. So in unbelief, Israel at the edge of the promise land retreated and they spent the next forty years wandering in the wilderness. They did not take God at His Word. They did not enjoy the victory that was promised. We have promises.

Our Lord has said the following, "The fields are white for harvest." (John 4:35)"The gospel of the kingdom shall go to all the world and then the end shall come." (Matt. 24:14) Do we believe these promises? Are we cowering like Israel or claiming them like David?

Num. 14:11 "The LORD said to Moses, "How long will these people treat me with contempt? How long will they refuse to believe in me, in spite of all the miraculous signs I have performed among them?" (NIV)

Has God given you a burden, a heart's desire, a dream that honors Him? Take His hand, claim His victory and step out in faith and watch Him honor your faith as He makes Himself known.

What follows next are five more positional truths that express the victories the Lord has promised.

28) <u>Victory Over the World – We are Overcomers</u>

> 1 John 5:**4, 5** "For whatever is born of God overcomes the world; and this is the victory that has overcome the world -our faith. Who is the one who overcomes the world, but he who believes that Jesus is the Son of God?"

What is love of the world? It is love of the world's good things, the fear of the world's laughter, mockery or blame. It is the secret desire to keep in favor with the world, the longing to do as others in the world do. Friendship with the world is being the enemy of God the Father.

> 1John 2:15 "Do not love the world nor the things in the world. If anyone loves the world, the love of the Father is not in him."

The Word says in Rom.12:2 "Do not be conformed to this world. But be transformed by the renewing of your mind, so that you may prove what the will of God is, that which is good and acceptable and perfect." We are living in a world designed to harm or hinder us with snares, traps, pitfalls and lures. It makes living the Christian life an uphill climb and it interrupts the work of the gospel and growth of Christian missions.

What does it mean to overcome the world? It means not sinking to the world's values. It means not embracing an unbiblical worldview. We must be content to be thought ill of by man when we please God. A fellow servant of Christ and friend, Tom Rode, has a challenge for each of us. Tom admonishes, "We should fear man far less, and fear God far more."

Each person has a worldview. It is one's belief system. This is the lens through which you see the world around you. Having a biblical worldview enables one to be an Overcomer. It is the lens through which you determine reality.

The following are major elements of a worldview.

1. Theology (What I believe about God): Does He exist? Is God personal? Can He be known?
2. Metaphysics (What is real?): Is there supernatural? What is the nature of ultimate reality? Is the universe sustained by God or is it self-existent?
3. Epistemology (How we gain knowledge.): Is truth relative? Is knowledge about the world possible? Can man trust his senses?
4. Ethics (Moral judgments): What is right and wrong? Are moral laws the same for all people?
5. Anthropology (The nature of the human being): Does man's existence end at death or is there an afterlife? Is man material only, or does he have a soul?

Is your worldview a Biblical worldview?
The Biblical worldview recognizes that:

1. God is three in one. That Jesus Christ is fully God and fully man. God created the universe ex-nihilo (out of nothing).
2. Christ followers believe that miracles are possible and that supernatural spirits exist.
3. Christ followers believe we can trust our senses, what we see, taste, smell, hear and touch is real and accurate. God is the source of absolute truth and the Bible is God's Word.
4. Further we believe that God is the measure and judge of reality and thus morality is universal and ultimate.
5. We also believe that man was made in the image of God. He therefore has an eternal soul, that after death he will spend eternity in either heaven or hell.

This is the worldview that gives us the most coherent picture of the world and gets us plugged into reality. This gives us the ability to have victory over the world.

Look at this example of overcoming the world by Daniel's three friends, Shadrack, Meshack and Abednego. We are going to see them obviously standing out alone against all peer pressure, refusing to bow to idols; for in their worldview there was only one God, their Lord God Yahweh. They had a confrontation with the Babylonian king Nebuchadnezzar. Nebuchadnezzar had just been told in Daniel's interpretation of his dream that he was the head of gold with regards to all other world empires. Taking that information quite a bit too far, he builds a ninety foot statue made of gold from head to foot. The statue was likely an image of Nebuchadnezzar himself. He assembles almost every leader under his rule on an open plain near his palace around the statue. When the band strikes up he expects them all to pay homage by bowing down in worship.

Can you imagine our three young men as they watch this statue under construction? "Oh guys this is not good. Our pagan king is having this made out of his expanded ego. You know what this means? We are going to have to worship this pagan deity or stand in opposition to the king". "You know, guys, it may cost us our lives". "Ya, but we can't dishonor Yahweh". When the music played they stood out bold on this open plain against the crowd as everyone bowed low but those three. Nebuchadnezzar was furious after he gave them a second chance to bow down threatening them with a furnace of fire if they continued in refusal.

Daniel 3:15-18 " Now when you hear the sound of the horn, flute, zither, lyre, harp, pipes and all kinds of music, if you are ready to fall down and worship the image I made, very good. But if you do not worship it, you will be thrown immediately into a blazing furnace. Then what god will be able to rescue you from my hand?" Shadrach, Meshach and Abednego replied to the king, "O Nebuchadnezzar, we do not need to defend ourselves before you in this matter. If we are thrown into the blazing furnace, the God we serve is able to save us from it, and he will rescue us from your hand, O king. But even if he does not, we want you to know, O king that we will not serve your gods or worship the image of gold you have set up. (NIV)"

Nebuchadnezzar was so furious; he could not believe anyone would defy him. Don't you love his boast, "What god is there who can deliver you out of my hands?" Our three young men stood their ground, replying, "Our God is able to deliver us. We believe He will and even if He doesn't, let it be known, we are not going to serve your gods or worship the golden image."

The king is in a rage and has the furnace heated seven times hotter. He has some of his chosen royal guard tie the young men up and throw them in the fire. This is costly because as these guards throw the guys in the furnace they themselves are engulfed and burn to death. Imagine the conversation between these young men. "We said the Lord could save us from the fire. I hope He hurries. What do you think he might do?" "Look at the king's face. He might have a stroke." "Do you think He will send a flood to quench the fire?" The Lord did not save them from the furnace. He saved them through the furnace. So many times we look to the Lord to rescue us from hardship. The Lord took them into the furnace and did two wonderful things. First, He personally joins them there in the furnace.

> Dan.3:21-25 "So these men, wearing their robes, trousers, turbans and other clothes, were bound and thrown into the blazing furnace. The king's command was so urgent and the furnace so hot that the flames of the fire killed the soldiers who took up Shadrach, Meshach and Abednego, and these three men, firmly tied, fell into the blazing furnace. Then King Nebuchadnezzar leaped to his feet in amazement and asked his advisers, "Weren't there three men that we tied up and threw into the fire?" They replied, "Certainly, O king." He said, "Look! I see four men walking around in the fire, unbound and unharmed, and the fourth looks like a son of the gods!"

He gets them alone to Himself without all the noise and hassle. Can't you just hear Him saying, "Thanks guys for standing up for me. Thanks for being willing to face this heat." Now second if you look at the text it says in three places that our guys went into the fire tied up. When they come out of the fire nothing has happened to them or their clothes. Their hair is not singed. They don't even have the smell of smoke on them. Only one thing has changed. They are no longer bound by that which bound them before they went through the fire.

The Lord did not deliver them *from* the trial, He delivered them *through* it. He was there in the midst of the trial and the only thing they lost was what bound them. That is a wonderful example of how you and I are able to overcome the world. We also can stand for Biblical truth rather than succumbing to the pressures of the world.

What kinds of golden statues does the world set up for us to worship and bow down to? We may bend the truth to look better to others. We may embrace the world's entertainment and become less discerning. We may compromise in business to make more money. We may go along with the crowd's values so we don't stick out. Instead, Believer, God sees everything about you. As an overcomer you live to please Him, not the world. As an overcomer you value integrity and honesty far more than the material goods of this temporal world. As an overcomer you hold on to the morals and values of Christlikeness and are proud to stand up for the Lord even though you may stick out.

Jesus said, in John's gospel.

John 16:33 "These things I have spoken to you, so that in Me you may have peace. In *the world* you have tribulation, but take courage; I have *overcome the world.*"

We need to dream dreams worthy of an overcomer, not intimidated by our circumstances or by people who might stand in the way and not afraid to be identified with our Lord and His values. For example one may look out and see there is no one in a certain people group or certain part of society who knows Jesus. There is a way into that people group with the good news if we will look for it and trust the Lord to open the door. We are overcomers. I am trusting the Lord to open a door into a country that is very dear to my heart. As I write, a major initiative into this country is just days away. I am trusting the Lord to raise up people in a very strategic role to come to faith and to influence the nation from their platform. You may have a dream. Maybe to see an unrighteous circumstance in your world righted. You may long to see the Lord use you to build into people's lives helping them have proper Biblical self-images. Do you face obstacles as you move toward your dreams? Remember, you are an overcomer, Citizen.

Jan is trusting the Lord to overcome in our daughter's life. Michelle, with her special needs, has had many difficulties with housing, home care, activities and medical care. It would be easy to feel defeated as we view all these obstacles, but Jan continues to dream, and work towards an optimal life for Michelle.

29) <u>Victory Over Sin – We can be undefeated</u>

> 1 Cor. 10:13 "No temptation has overtaken you but such as is common to man; and God is faithful, who will not allow you to be tempted beyond what you are able, but with the temptation will provide the way of escape also, so that you will be able to endure it."

> Rom. 6:12,13 "Therefore do not let sin reign in your mortal body so that you obey its lusts, and do not go on presenting the members of your body to sin as instruments of unrighteousness; but present yourselves to God as those alive from the dead, and your members as instruments of righteousness to God."

When I sin whose fault is it? *My fault!* It was my choice. I wanted to commit that sin and therefore did not even look for the way of escape. I presented my body as an instrument of unrighteousness. You may remember how earlier I presented the idea that one's body is a weapon. If one chooses to use it for unrighteousness, it is like throwing one's body into the fray to be used by the enemy against oneself and others. When I present myself to sin I harm the home team. I engage in friendly fire.

How does temptation differ from sin? First, to be tempted is not a sin. Temptation is a lure. It is a thought or even something that actually passes before our senses. Usually it is something that attracts our eyes, ears, taste, smell or touch. These can all arouse desire in us. We do not sin until we choose to yield to the temptation. Sin is choosing against God's will as expressed in His Word. We are choosing our will above His desire and saying, "I believe I know what is best, what is right for me."

Second when tempted what should I expect? I can expect to be able to choose not to sin, that God is faithful to provide a way of escape with each and every temptation.

I was a catcher when I played baseball. Wanting to win, I would memorize the other team's lineup and all their players' tendencies. I would examine how they responded to each pitch they faced. Like many I hate to lose. I had to find a way to take advantage of any weakness I saw. We had to beat them. You and I have got to believe we can be undefeated as we face each temptation; however my problem comes when I don't care if I lose the battle. If I can have that winning attitude as an athlete, I can certainly approach sin that way. What a shame when I don't! What a shame when you don't!

The life of a believer is designed to be a life of sustained victory over sin. God can give us a heart to see the exceeding sinfulness of sin in the sight of our holy precious perfect One. Do we ever have to experience defeat? Not according to the Lord's promise! You have a promised victory. You can have the same attitude about your sin as the Lord does. You can be undefeated!

30) <u>Victory Over the Devil –He has been rendered powerless</u>

> Heb. 2:14 "Therefore, since the children share in flesh and blood, He Himself likewise also partook of the same, that through death He might render powerless him who had the power of death, that is, the devil."

Life is very confusing if you do not take into account that there is a villain, that you, My Friend, have an enemy. He is a villain who hates your heart and wants to destroy you. There is a dark power in the universe, a mighty evil spirit who is the power behind death, disease and sin. He never sleeps, nor slumbers. He does not go on holiday or take a vacation. His goal is to be seen as an angel of light so he can seduce us, deceive us and assault us. He is the unseen enemy who is always going about seeking someone to devour. He is spying out all our ways, discovering our weaknesses. He is a murderer and a liar from the very beginning.

In time of war it is the worst mistake to underestimate your enemy or to belittle the conflict. Do not think that you have the option to remain neutral or sit it out in the war. There is no armistice or truce. We are in a war for the souls of all mankind. It is a fight of absolute necessity and universal importance.

The devil has been in the business of deceiving men and woman for many thousands of years, and he knows exactly how to approach every human soul. That rather galls me. How about you? He is the best liar, manipulator, psychologist, salesman, ad agent and seducer. What are his weapons in this warfare? He uses doubt, guilt, temptation and lies. We covered temptation in the positional truth just above. So let's think through *doubt*, *lies* and *guilt* below.

He creates *doubt* about our security, acceptance and forgiveness. You know, things like, "I am so terrible. How could the Lord really accept me?" He throws in doubt about our position in Christ. What do you think is the source of that doubt? The devil loves to have us doubt the Lord's character and His Word.

The devil uses the wounds we have received throughout our lives to cause us to believe *lies* about ourselves or about people in our lives. We can believe the lie that we are not worthy, interesting, capable or smart enough. The enemy accuses "How can you do that and think you're a Christian? You really aren't loved by God."

The Lord convicts us of sin so that we will recognize it as sin. We then need to turn from that particular behavior. We confess it and move forward. The Lord desires us to have a clean conscience once we have received His forgiveness. If *guilt* or shame remains, that is the enemy's tool to affect our self-worth to cause us to feel unusable.

In each of the enemy's tactics our response should be to verbalize truth to ourselves and to him. God's Word is our greatest weapon. As Neil Anderson explains:

"Freedom from spiritual conflict and bondage is not a power encounter; it is a truth encounter. Satan is a deceiver, and he will work undercover at all costs. But the truth of God's Word exposes him and his lie. His demons are like cockroaches that scurry for the shadows when the light comes on. Satan's power is in the lie, and when his lie is exposed by the truth, his plans are foiled. ...truth is the liberating agent. The power of Satan is in the lie, and the power of the believer is in knowing the truth."

John 8:32 "You shall know the truth, and the truth shall set you free."

John 17:15, 17 "I do not ask Thee to take them out of the world, but to keep them from the Evil one....Sanctify them in Thy truth; Thy Word is truth."

His truth combats lies. His truth embraced removes doubt. His truth believed cleanses our heart of guilt and shame.

What kind of lion roars? One that is weak and toothless. Its goal is merely to scare the victim. The old toothless lion roars in order to move his prey in the direction where the real danger lies. The predator ready to pounce is very quiet. He wants to sneakily deceive us with lies, doubt and guilt.

1 Peter 5:8 "Be of sober spirit, be on the alert. Your adversary, the devil, prowls around like a roaring lion, seeking someone to devour."

Our enemy the devil does not have the power to destroy us unless we yield to his lies, doubts, guilt and fear. We have the authority of Jesus. We are told in the Word to "flee lust" and "resist the Devil". Most of us have it backward. We try to resist temptation and we flee the Devil.

We enter the enemy's turf in one of two places. One place is the realms he has inspired and where we have no business going, certain places of entertainment, programs on television or places on the internet. The enemy will find our area of weakness. That lion can act like a pet cat who will purr asking for his belly to be scratched and then as we reach out to scratch him he devours the arm. We are called to stay away from this turf. The other place we encounter the enemy is in the arena of evangelism. Here we are entering his turf to rescue the perishing. We are commanded to go forth here. Many times he creates barriers, difficulties and distractions when we are engaged in evangelism. You are called to be a soldier facing these challenges. We are to be alert and diligent.

1 John 4:4 "You are from God, little children, and have overcome them; because greater is He who is in us than he who is in the world."

Rom. 8:31 "If God is for us who can be against us?"

Frankly if someone is against us then so what, because He is for us and we are promised victory. Expect that and take the battle to Him. It glorifies God. Remember the Devil has been rendered powerless.

31) <u>Victory Over Circumstances – "Undaunted"</u>

Rom. 8:28 "We know that God works all things together for good for the ones who love God, for those who are called according to his purpose." (CEB)

There is no question that many of the things that happen in our lives are not good. Many actually are horribly bad. God has promised you, dear brother or sister that He will bring about good from those circumstances.

Jesus came that we might have life and have it abundantly. All of us have rotten experiences and difficult situations throughout our lives. If I am an unbeliever I just have lousy circumstances. In contrast, as a believer, I don't simply have trouble but with those troubles I have the opportunity to: 1. glorify God, 2. further His kingdom, 3. earn eternal rewards, 4. please Him, 5. see my character built, 6. see God's provision, 7. comfort others, and 8. become more like Christ. There is reason, meaning and purpose as a result and that's part of the abundant life.

The Lord's personal touch is upon our lives. He designs these touches just for us. Circumstances and trials do not have the final word. God will use whatever circumstance occurs to bring about

109

good. You have likely heard people respond to the question, "How are you?" with, "Well, under the circumstances I'm doing okay." I think our Lord's response would be, "What are you doing *under* the circumstances? Take my hand .We are going to get on top of this."

I made a friend that I would see usually three times a year when I would visit the University of Toledo. His name is Bernie. Bernie is a quadriplegic. Bernie had trouble for many years communicating with people. He carried a board that he could hang on the back of his chair and when someone wished to talk with him he would touch a pencil which he held in his mouth on individual letters and spell out words. This was difficult and time consuming and at times Bernie would be embarrassed because he would drool on the board.

Bernie had some pretty deep insights on life. He would share those insights with people who would take the time to talk. There was never a sense of anger or bitterness as you would talk with him because Bernie knew Jesus and Jesus had given Bernie a dear heart. He had his testimony of how he trusted Christ typed out to give to folks to share about himself. He was thrilled when someone worked it out for him to receive a computer which he could take with him and use from his chair. This made communication so much easier.

In one of our conversations, Bernie opened his heart and told me how at times he wrestled with sadness knowing he would never have a girlfriend. He found himself grieving over his limitations. He honestly shared how he wrestled with being jealous of those who were not like him. As Bernie grew in his walk with the Lord he gained an eternal perspective I encouraged him to write a book sharing many of his thoughts, joys and experiences. He longs to be able to touch people with his story. He hopes to have an eternal impact.

Bernie has a special love for the Lord. He so looks forward to the day when He will run and sing and play an instrument in eternity. He has a wonderful hope. Here in this body Bernie is still undaunted. He has an abundant life because of Jesus. He has many friends who go out of their way to see that Bernie gets to places and is cared for. His friends care for him giving him opportunity to go on weekend retreats. He has participated in Special Olympics and done quite well in his events and he gets greatly excited when he talks about it. To meet Him and talk with him would minister to your heart.

Here is a man who has victory over his circumstances. You have a promise from the Lord of victory over your circumstances. You can live undaunted.

32) <u>Victory Over Fear – We can be fearless</u>

1John 4:18 "There is no fear in love; but perfect love casts out fear, because fear involves punishment, and the one who fears is not perfected in love."

We are secure in His love. There is no fear of His disapproval, and no fear of judgment, harm or consequences. We can rest in the finished work of Christ. Because of His love we do not fear our past or our past sins. His perfect love has cast out the fear of rejection.

When my daughter Michelle was small she would do some pretty surprising things. She would climb up on a table and with just this simple warning, "Daddy catch me"! She would leap head and face first toward me. I would turn quickly and thankfully I never missed catching her. She would take these crazy risks though we pleaded with her to stop. She did this no less than a hundred times in child-hood. Thankfully she did stop sometime before her sixth birthday. Why was she so fearless? She didn't feel she could be hurt. She had the belief that "Daddy will always catch me". What a wonderful heart. Our hearts need to feel that same way toward our Lord. This is a trust that is worthy of being expressed about God's perfect love.

In the security of this perfect love we are able to attempt to honor the Lord and accomplish tasks for Him without the fear of failure or the fear of our personal weaknesses. I was asked to be one of the speakers to the major Science professors of a major university in Eastern Europe. We were asked to make a presentation for God being the creator of all. We were doing this before men and women who had just come out of an atheistic state and there were a lot of reasons to be scared or intimidated before these men and women. We had prepared ourselves with classes in our fields, for my partner it was chemistry and for me it was worldviews and philosophy. We claimed Mattew 10:18-20 "and you will even be brought before governors and kings for My sake, as a testimony to them and to the Gentiles. But when they hand you over, do not worry about how or what you are to say; for it will be given you in that hour what you are to say. For it is not you who speak, but it is the Spirit of your Father who speaks in you".

We felt we couldn't fail because perfect love casts out fear. How could we fail? The Lord would be pleased that we were stepping out in faith. The Spirit of Truth would empower us and open some hearts. Some would accept what we shared and some would not. Our explanation of how many discoveries in science pointed more to a personal designer then it did to random chance and quoting many philosophers of the past like Plato and Aristotle caused them to respond positively and quite a few of them said, "I have always felt there was more and now that we are free to believe in God I want you to know I do." Our presentation was certainly not flawless and there are far better people to address the issues. But we were there and the opportunity presented itself, so we said, "Father catch us!" We were taking a leap of faith.

We are dearly valuable to the Lord. The hairs on our heads are numbered. He has told us a sparrow cannot fall to the ground without His knowledge and that we are more valuable than many sparrows. For us there is not fear of lack because of His promises. We are not vulnerable. We are not unprotected. Because of the Lord's perfect love we have no fear of abandonment. We are not alone or without His support. Fear is cast out further as Jesus says in John 14: 1-3, "Do not let your heart be troubled," and then goes on to tell us we will be with Him in heaven in a place he is personally preparing for us.

According to the degree of his faith, the Christian fights well or poorly, wins victories or suffers occasional setbacks. Nothing makes the anxieties of warfare sit so lightly on a person as the assurance of Christ's love and continual protection. Nothing enables us to bear the weariness of the battle, the struggling and the wrestling against sin like the unshakeable confidence that Jesus is on our side and success is sure. We can be fearless.

33) <u>Freedom and Liberation</u>

Gal. 5:1, "It was for freedom that Christ has set you free, therefore keep standing firm and do not be subject again to a yoke of slavery."

2 Cor. 3:17 "Now the Lord is the Spirit, and where the Spirit of the Lord is there is liberty."

What does Paul mean when he speaks of freedom? It implies first of all deliverance. We can be rescued and set free from an accusing conscience. We can be rescued from the power of sin and the curse which the law pronounces upon a sinner.

Secondly, it implies our glorious endowment of access to the Father in Sonship and the liberty of walking in the Spirit. This is grace, not performance. It is the freedom to fail, not the freedom from failure. It is the ability to accept oneself and others with all our weaknesses.

None of us enjoy being with people who hover over us, waiting for us to fail. We can appreciate constructive criticism, but we do struggle with disapproval. We all want to please people who have authority over us. When this happens, we tend to find acceptance by performing for people rather than rejecting legalism and live by grace.

The law creeps into our lives. This happens because we feel we are under certain standards. You can probably remember someone in your life who relished correcting your every mistake. When this happens, we become tense and anticipate our own failure. When people scrutinize every move, we become uncomfortable and if anything, we are probably more prone to mistakes than we would be otherwise. This is because not making mistakes becomes the focus.

Sometimes, the source of performance in my life is not from others but from me. I mentally create a phantom or super Christian whose life I measure against my own. Perhaps I am a perfectionist having to have all the answers, or feeling the need to say yes to every ministry opportunity. We can put ourselves under a standard of performance without the help of anyone else.

When we live under the law, the result is often discouragement, disapproval and lack of initiative. I remember a period of months in which I felt so discouraged that I would do things I knew not to be best just to avoid conflict. I would know the correct direction to turn or the right decision to make. But if someone would say turn this way or I think this is what we should do, I would yield immediately. My fear of being wrong was so great that I was reluctant to take any risks because I feared the consequences, even when I truly felt I was right. I remember driving with Jan and taking a left turn at her request that I knew to be wrong just because I did not want to discuss it and find out that I just might be mistaken. It was easier to live with the risk of someone else being wrong than my being wrong. Fear caused me to shrink back. I lacked confidence and creativity. As a result, I withdrew. I led poorly because I believed I was under the law. What a far cry from how my dad raised me.

My dad was my baseball coach. He firmly believed that kids play baseball not to build up the ego of a coach but to learn to enjoy baseball. Whenever the kids were up to bat my dad had a policy of "no-walking." Since this was not the seventh game of the World Series, there was going to be none of this crouching down and not swinging. We were there to play and learn the game.

During the first few games of the season, the kids might swing and miss. My dad would say, "Hey great swing! That was nice and level, Little Guy! Way to go! Good cut, good eye!" Then the kid would swing and miss again and my dad would say "Hey, you chose the right one to swing at!" "Way to go Little Buddy!" They'd strike out and you know what they would feel? Not that they failed, because what was emphasized was not that they failed, but that they were getting better. They couldn't wait to get up to bat again. The next time they were at bat, they might foul off a pitch and my dad would be right there yelling, "All right, you got a piece of it! Way to go!"

When kids got home, parents would ask, "How did you do?" And the kid would say, "Well, I fouled off two today. Coach was really pleased with my swing. I struck out but I'm doing great."

At the next game, the kid might be thrown out at first base, but my dad would meet him at the base and say, "All right, that was great! Great swing, good job! You really straightened that one out." They might quibble, "Coach, I made an out." He would remind them, "No, you're getting better and better!" The response was often, "But Mr. Sylvester, we're losing". Dad just smiled and told them, "Oh no, no, no! You're really learning how to play this game."

When a kid got his first hit, you know where he'd look? At my dad, right! My dad came unglued when they grounded out, so they could hardly wait to see what he'd do when they actually got a hit. He'd give them a smile, and thumbs up, and a proud nod all the while as he was clapping.

On my Dad's teams we were better friends and had more fun than any team in the league. Our habit seemed to be that we'd lose our first two or three games of the season, and then we'd win all the rest.

I believe this is the way Jesus would coach. And this is the way I see Jesus work in lives. With this picture of Jesus we are free to take challenges. We are free to ask questions. We don't have to know everything. We are free to step out in faith without the fear of failure. Now that is liberating.

34) <u>The Armor of God</u>

Eph. 6:**11-17** (NIV) "Put on the full armor of God so that you can take your stand against the devil's schemes. For our struggle is not against flesh and blood, but against the rulers, against the authorities, against the powers of this dark world and against the spiritual forces of evil in the heavenly realms Therefore put on the full armor of God, so that when the day of evil comes, you may be able to stand your ground, and after you have done everything, to stand. Stand firm then, with the belt of truth buckled around your waist, with the breastplate of righteousness in place, and with your feet fitted with the readiness that comes from the gospel of peace In addition to all this, take up the shield of faith, with which you can extinguish all the flaming arrows of the evil one. Take the helmet of salvation and the sword of the Spirit, which is the word of God."

Our picture of military strength here is battle readiness. You and I are in a warzone. If I believe that I won't be so prone to relax. I won't believe I am not under threat and act like I can get comfortable. I won't sit around in lounge clothes as opposed to God's armor.

A very motivating factor to me is realizing that the enemy, Satan, has limited resources. It is an exciting thought to me that at the beginning of the school year for example, so much ministry launches in schools all over the world. At university after university and high school after high school believers return to campus and the student ministries on those campuses move forward with great plans and initiative to reach incoming students with the gospel. In public schools all across the globe many teachers who have been trained to use curriculum based on the Scriptures greet a new classroom of students in the fall. In other words believers armed with the gospel simultaneously move forward by faith in great numbers taking the message of Christ to these audiences. The enemy is limited. He gets spread thin. He can only get his resistance to just so many places.

Let me review again a way to see this, for some of us we will run into greater resistance and see smaller results. But we have drawn his forces and we have occupied the enemy. In other places his defense is weaker and as a result large numbers respond to the good news. All of us have engaged the enemy. Some have had major breakthroughs. Others by advancing with the gospel may not be breaking through enemy lines as easily but are part of the advance just as much.

In this spiritual warfare we need to recognize that we are given as one of those forty positional truths, the armor of God. I have the breast plate of righteousness to protect my heart. I have the shield of faith to extinguish the accusations of the evil one, by believing God's truth. I have the helmet of salvation and I am protected by my security in Christ which wards off the enemy's attempts to flaunt my failures in my face. I have my feet shod with the gospel of peace to be able to maneuver through tough terrain and have secure footing as I share the gospel. I have the sword of the Spirit which is the Word of God to answer attacks like the Lord did with His temptations. Satan is vanquished; Jesus is King. This is what you and I are a part of. There is not a better time to be alive. God is doing something wonderfully historic in this day.

Notice all the armor is for the front of our bodies. There is no armor for the back. The Lord's soldier is going forward into battle.

Jesus said, "The gates of hell shall not prevail against us". He wants to rescue the perishing. We enter enemy territory when we are involved in evangelism. Think of where God has placed you and view it like Israel entering the Promised Land. Remember the promises God gave to Joshua.

Joshua 1:2-5 "Moses my servant is dead. Now then ... I will give you every place where you set your foot, as I promised Moses. ... No one will be able to stand up against you all the days of your life. As I was with Moses, so I will be with you; I will never leave you nor forsake you. "Be strong and courageous, because you will lead these people to inherit the land I swore to their forefathers to give them." (NIV)

Well, just like Joshua and Israel the Lord has given us promises for our time and our part of His world.

Matt. 28:18-20 "And Jesus came up and spoke to them, saying, "All authority has been given to Me in heaven and on earth. "Go therefore and make disciples of all the nations, baptizing them in the name of the Father and the Son and the Holy Spirit, teaching them to observe all that I commanded you; and lo, I am with you always, even to the end of the age."

Acts 1:8 "but you will receive power when the Holy Spirit has come upon you; and you shall be My witnesses both in Jerusalem, and in all Judea and Samaria, and even to the remotest part of the earth."

Picture the place where God has placed you as Joshua would. Pray for it and claim it for your King! Go in and take possession of it in the strength and armor of your Lord.

35) Identification – co-crucified, co-buried, co-raised

Rom. 5:3-5 "Or do you not know that all of us who have been baptized into Christ Jesus have been *baptized into His death*? Therefore we have been buried with Him through baptism into death, so that as Christ was raised from the dead through the glory of the Father, so we too might walk in newness of life. For if we have become united with Him in the likeness of His death, certainly we shall also be in the likeness of His resurrection." (emphasis mine)

I learned this last principle in this section at a weekend with Josh McDowell.

Josh was teaching from the book of Romans. He was sharing his series "The Revolutionary Revelation" from chapters one through eight in Romans. He explained the principle of identification especially as it was explained in chapter six. This is not a wet baptism that Paul is talking about here. For example, when dipping a paint brush into a bucket of blue paint the brush is now baptized, not because the brush is wet but because the brush is now blue. It is identified with the paint. Soldiers before a battle would dip their swords in blood to symbolize what they were identifying with what would take place in the next moments. We have been identified with Christ. As he was crucified, we were crucified with Him.

When Jesus died, we died together with Him. When Christ rose from the dead, we rose with Him. When Christ ascended to heaven, we ascended with Him and are *now* seated with Him in the heavenly places. Our identification with Christ is so complete that God reckons us as having experienced co-crucifixion, co-burial, co-resurrection, co-ascension and co-glorification. Spiritually you were there with Christ. This is the way God sees us. Then, should we not see ourselves in the same manner?

Christ broke sin's power over you. Even so consider (that is reckon, be constantly counting upon this fact) yourselves to be dead to sin, but alive to God in Christ Jesus. We are no longer obligated to serve the old sin master. Paul says, "For he who has died is freed from sin." (Rom. 6:7) The obligation to sin has been shattered. Dead men are no longer slaves.

The burial of Christ was an historical fact, and our burial with Him is a spiritual truth to be acted on. Sadly we go around like a yard dog digging up old buried bones instead of leaving the dead buried. We go digging around in old sins, and temptations looking where we ought not to look. Leave the dead buried. My sin nature not only died, but it was buried as well.

In Romans 6:1-11 Paul teaches that we live in our position when we first *know* these truths, then *reckon,* count these as reality (confirm these in my beliefs) and then *present* ourselves to acts of righteousness consistent with our position.

We are to KNOW the truths of our position. We should memorize each of these truths. Next RECKON, embrace the fact that God sees you as righteous as Jesus. Count on the reality that you are a joint-heir with Christ. Live in, confirm in your heart, count on, and reckon that you have the power of Christ's resurrection at your disposal. PRESENT yourself, your body to the rights of citizenship. Claim the truths of your position and present your body to the exercise of that truth. You have the authority of a believer, so live in it, count on it and present yourself to the righteous acts of one with authority.

Josh McDowell was speaking at a major university to 5,000 people in a large ballroom sharing his evangelistic lecture on male/female relationships. Down the center aisle advanced a group of men. They raised a murmur in the crowd because they were eerily dressed, completely in black and adorned with spooky jewelry. It was obvious their intention was to be alarming, threatening and disruptive. They were Satanists. Josh had lost the attention of the audience.

He swallowed hard, and he remembered the truth of his identity in Christ as the Holy Spirit prompted his mind that, "He was co-crucified, co-buried, co-raised and seated at the right hand of power." So Josh addressed them, "Excuse me Gentlemen what is it that you want?" They railed back insults! They cursed! They blasphemed God!

Josh thought again, "I am co-crucified, co-buried, co-raised and seated at the right hand of power." Josh quoted Scripture. He declared Christ and shared the gospel. It went back and forth. Finally, the leader of the Satanists shouted, "Mister what makes you so sure!" Josh shot back, "The authority of God's Word!" "And who do you think you are?" the leader challenged. "I am a child of the King, His chosen son and I am co-crucified, co-buried, co-risen with Christ, seated at the right hand of power on high in Christ!" he triumphantly declared.

The group of men stood there befuddled, thwarted and powerless. Not sure what to do, they looked at each other turned and walked away. As they got to the side door; the leader turned and addressed Josh a final time, "Mister, you may have won this time, but the next time the victory will be ours!" Josh turned and pronounced, "Oh no it won't be, for I am co-crucified, co-buried, co-raised and seated at the right hand of power on high!" Defeated, speechless they turned and walked out the door. Their boss had no authority to handle this.

I am sitting in my chair listening as Josh is sharing this story and in my heart I am saying, "Yeah! Yeah! That's it! That is what we are able to do from our position in Christ. That is what the Word says about us as believers. That is the authority of our position! We are called to be revolutionaries. We are seated in the heavenlies in Christ. We are the Church! 'The gates of hell shall not prevail against us'! I have got to grasp this. I have got to understand this.

I made it my purpose to understand positional truth. I studied the Scriptures and color-coded my Bible with a special color for every verse that related to our position in Christ. I discovered these forty things that happened to us the instant we became Christians. We need to know these truths, reckon them to be true and present ourselves according to our identity in Christ.

Let's live in our position, claiming these promises, our identity and these rights.

Will you? Will you hunger to be what God has called us to be, made us to be? Citizen you have God's promises. Live in your position in Christ. Exercise your rights as you confront and face opposition. This is for the glory of God. We draw on these truths not to satisfy our own egos, but it honors God when we live in our position and it is God who gets the credit. We step out in faith drawing on our position in Christ all for the glory of God.

POSITIONAL TRUTH SERIES
CHAPTER #6

—✦✦✦—

<u>Royalty</u>

We are continuing with the meatier concepts of understanding in this last section of our positional truth and will now look into our *regality*. You have "Throne Room Privileges". Let's look at what these involve.

A leader of a western nation needed to meet with a most powerful monarch of an Asian country. Time was set for him to make his petition, but before he could be permitted access to the monarch he had to be instructed in the protocol and customs of entry to the throne. One must not offend the throne. One must remember the power wielded by the throne. And one must show the respect due the throne all at the peril of one's life.

There were all of these areas of homage that must be observed. The diplomat needed to be aware of how he should enter, of how he should dress and how he should demonstrate proper fear. He would need to learn how to cast his eyes, how his head needed to be bowed, how he could never show his back, how when he approaches he must always shuffle never stride and then only when asked a question may he speak.

To demonstrate respect and humility and to be properly trained the diplomat arrived days early. After much pomp and circumstance and excessive diplomacy, at last the foreign dignitary was to realize his opportunity. Permission was granted for an audience with the monarch to request a daylong hearing.

He entered after being formally announced. Slowly he approached shuffling his feet with back bent, his head lowered and his eyes fixed to the floor. As he reached the rugs and pillows before the throne he prostrated himself with arms extended and with his face in the pillows.

A squeal was heard from the back of the room. A shout of glee resounded, and a seven year old boy bounded into the room. He ran to the throne, leapt into the monarch's lap, and wrapped his arms around his neck. The beloved son and crown prince found no need for ceremony or decorum. He was welcomed!

Which one are you, son or diplomat? Which of these approaches is evident in your life? Are you ready for this set of positional truths?

36) <u>Confident Access to God</u>

Eph. 3:8-12 „To me, the very least of all saints, this grace was given, to preach to the Gentiles the unfathomable riches of Christ, and to bring to light what is the administration of the mystery which for ages has been hidden in God who created all things; so that the manifold wisdom of God might now be made known through the church to the rulers and the authorities in the heavenly places. This was in accordance with the eternal purpose which He carried out in Christ Jesus our Lord, <u>in whom we have boldness and confident access through faith in Him.</u>"

What If the president of the United States were to give you a solid hour of his full attention? Along with that, he was desirous of hearing your evaluation of current situations, the needs you perceived and conditions you felt needed to be changed and he promised to move all the resources of the United States to bear on your requests. What would you do? Do you think you would make the time to meet with him? Imagine, would you not be thrilled with the opportunity? Do you think you might take the time seriously? Would you present your heart and ideas carefully and thoughtfully?

Is this not our privilege and more with our Lord?

Rom. 8: 32 "He who did not spare His own Son, but delivered Him over for us all, how will He not also with Him freely give us all things?"

You and I can take all our concerns, all of our friends and loved ones, all of our burdens and problems to Him. Who cares more for what is on your heart than the Lord? Is there anyone or anything that could bring more to your concerns? Does it strike you this way?

John Piper would remind us that when we come to the Lord that we are not placing long distance phone calls, we are whispering in His ear. Nor are we lounging in our parlors merely ringing for the butler, but we are on the front lines speaking with the commander-in-chief updating Him on the progress and needs of the battle.

Before her first birthday our daughter Chelle required open heart surgery. Let me give you a little more of the details. The night before surgery the nurse walked us through what our dear one would undergo. They would open her chest, split her ribs, chill her blood so that her heart would slow to a stop so that they could reroute her blood supply through their machines. The surgeon could then work on her heart which would need to be opened and repaired.

Then the nurse introduced us to the surgeon's pastor who met with every parent of a child who was to have surgery. He informed us that the surgeon considered his role and his hands as servants of the Lord. That was wonderful to discover. You can imagine how apprehensive Jan and I were about what our daughter would face the next morning. That information sure helped.

That next morning we handed our precious daughter into the attending nurse's arms. With tears seeping out of the corners of our eyes we walked to the waiting room that had a chapel attached to it. Jan and I walked through a crowded waiting room of many other parents with children in surgery at that moment, and we were surprised we had an empty chapel all to ourselves. The chapel was larger than the smoked filled waiting room with noisy televisions. In that great sanctuary we crawled into our Lord Jesus' lap and walked through every stage of that operation. We spent four hours alone with Him in that chapel. We were nervous but comforted as we pictured Jesus guiding the surgeon's hands. We were able spend four hours in the arms of the Lord whispering in His ear.

We came to find that Chelle's hole in her heart was larger than anyone expected and there were unexpected complications. The surgeon we had was one of only three men in the country who could have performed the operation. You can believe we rejoiced with Jesus watching her motoring around her crib a week later at home. That was a whole week earlier than predicted. Confident access to the Lord and whispering in His ear sure changed our perspective on life's challenges.

37) The Royal Priesthood

In the book of Hebrews Jesus is shown to be superior to anything Judaism could boast. He is superior to angels, to Joshua's rest, to Moses, to the old covenant, to Aaron's priesthood and to the Old Covenant sacrificial system. Jesus' priesthood is like that of Melchizedek. Melchizedek is the royal priest to whom Abraham paid tithes. The writer of Hebrews tells us that this was in recognition of the superiority of his priesthood to the one that would follow through Aaron known as the Levitical priesthood. Melchizedek is both a King who rules and a priest who intercedes before God for men.

> 2 Peter 2:9 "But you are A CHOSEN RACE, A royal PRIESTHOOD, A HOLY NATION, A PEOPLE FOR God's OWN POSSESSION, so that you may proclaim the excellencies of Him who has called you out of darkness into His marvelous light ";

We approach the throne of God seated in Christ and standing in His righteousness. We enter with bold confidence that our prayers are heard and answered. We are those priests who are able to minister to others having the ministry of reconciliation as ambassadors of Christ. As royal priests we claim victory because the gates of hell shall not prevail for we are the church triumphant.

You are able to minister to others. You are able to help people experience the reality of their personal savior Jesus. He corrects the lies they have heard over and over in their minds. You are a royal priest.

38) Promised Answered Prayer

Sometimes the Lord does some special things to plant a Biblical truth deep within us. Our children experience our prayers for them as we tuck them in at night. They hear us pray for them when they are ill. With every meal we thank the Lord for His graciousness to us. We pray with them for people that they know and love.

In our family there was something wonderfully vivid concerning this with Dan's first heartfelt prayer when he was just around four. His very special blanket that he had slept with every night of his life was lost. There was no putting him to bed. We had looked for an hour, then tried to put him to bed without it but there was no consoling him. So with him we looked for another fifteen, twenty minutes. Then at last, I said "Dan, let's ask Jesus to find your blanket." So in his sweet voice in his own words he asked Jesus to find this most precious possession. Not ten seconds later we opened a closet door and for no explainable reason there was the blanket. The Lord answered my son's first real prayer immediately and poignantly. I believe that has shaped his heart toward prayer ever since. What is your experience with answered prayer?

John 14:13, 14 "Whatever you ask in My name, that will I do, so that the Father may be glorified in the Son. If you ask Me anything in My name, I will do it."

Why is the Lord going to answer our prayer? It will glorify the Father. That's right. It is good publicity as to the greatness and goodness of our God. Answered prayer is a part of the Lord's public relations. We are to be known for His answers to our prayers. Are you? If a believer is not seeing answered prayer, he or she is cheating the Father out of this opportunity for Him to be glorified. We are invited to ask anything that is in accordance with the character of our Lord and that approaches God's throne not on our authority but according to the power and authority of Christ.

What are the conditions in Scripture that lead to answered prayer?

John 15: 7 "If you abide in Me, and My words abide in you, ask whatever you wish, and it will be done for you."

Abiding in Christ is walking in the Spirit. It is living in your new nature or walking in the light. His word abiding in us is "letting the word of Christ richly dwell within us" Col.3:16. I believe this idea is further clarified by Psalm 37:4 "Delight yourself in the Lord; and He will give you the desires of your heart." As we allow the Word of God to renew our minds the Lord will be the One who places the desires he wants into our hearts. We then are free to ask for what is on our hearts, "whatever you wish", the Lord told us. What I believe this means is in answer to our prayers the Lord will either change the situation or clearly change us. So we continue to ask until one or the other occurs.

As a young believer I was encouraged to keep a "God box". I would write my prayers on three by five cards, date the requests and place them in a card file box. When God answered the prayer I then recorded the answer to the prayer on the same card, dated it and put it in a second box. It was this one I called my "God box".

You know I could barely keep up with the Lord. I enjoyed showing guys I was sharing the gospel with my fists full of answered prayer. Especially as part of answering their question, "How do you know this stuff is true?" "Well", I would say, "it is hard to ignore that each of these cards is an answer to my personal requests of the Lord." I use a journal now though I must confess I am not as diligent as I was those first few years and that is to my great loss.

1 John 5:14, 15 "This is the confidence which we have before Him, that, if we ask anything according to His will, He hears us. And if we know that He hears us in whatever we ask, we know that we have the requests which we have asked from Him"

We need to confidently ask of the Lord consistent with these conditions and expect we will receive our requests. The Lord is quite able to handle His own reputation. You may pray for something year after year. Continue to pursue the Lord as He commanded us to do in his parable of the women and the unrighteous judge Luke 18; 1-8. In this parable He shares that at all times we ought to pray and not to lose heart. So keep praying knowing that the Lord will change what you are asking for or He will clearly change the desire of your heart.

James tells us in 4:2 "You do not have because you do not ask."

If I am abiding in Christ and His Word is abiding in me and I am praying about things consistent with His character and through His authority, I believe I am praying according to His will and therefore know that He hears me and will grant the requests I have asked from Him.

1 John 5:14, 15 "This is the confidence which we have before Him, that, if we ask anything according to His will, He hears us. And if we know that He hears us in whatever we ask, we know that we have the requests which we have asked from Him.

We have the promise of answered prayer.

39) <u>Seated with Christ in the Heavenlies</u>

Eph. 2:6 "and raised us up with Him, and seated us with Him in the heavenly places in Christ Jesus",

I received a card in the mail. On the front of the card it read in bold letters, *"Don't look up, look down"*. I turned the page and looked inside, It read, "Because you are seated in Christ in heavenly places, it is time to see things from God's perspective, from His point of view."

This is how radically wonderful the New Covenant is in comparison to the Old Covenant. We have a high priest who is seated in the holy of holies of heaven. Positionally we are placed in Him. In the old system the high priest could only enter the holy of holies once a year for just minutes. He could not pause to enjoy the Lord's presence or marvel at how the Shekina was especially awe inspiring that day.

He could never sit down. In fact a rope was tied around his ankle and a bell would ring as he moved, for should he violate the sanctity of that holy of holies by violating the Lord's prescribed instructions, he would be struck dead. No one could go in after him; they would have to pull him out.

In helping you understand these incredible *throne room privileges* of the church age, I would like to share the following story, which is from John Phillips' "Exploring Hebrews".

Imagine a man from the nation of Moab, a Moabite of old gazing down upon the tents and tabernacle of Israel from an excellent vantage point on a mountain.

He is attracted by what he sees. So he descends the mountain to the plain and walks toward the sacred walls that surround and enclose the tabernacle. The walls are over his head and therefore all is unseeable. He walks around until he comes to the gate where he sees a man.

He asks the man, "May I go in there?" pointing through the gate to where the bustle of activity in the tabernacle outer court could be seen.

"Who are you?" demands the man suspiciously for any Israelite would know he could go in there.

"I am a man from Moab", the stranger replies.

Well, says the man at the gate, I am very sorry, but you cannot go in there. It's not for you. The Law of Moses has barred the Moabite (actually all gentiles) from any part in the worship of Israel until his tenth generation.

Looking very sad he asks, "What would I have to do to be able to go in there?"

"Well frankly Sir, you would have to be born again, you would have to be born an Israelite. You would need to be born of the tribe of Judah, or of the tribe of Benjamin, or let's say Dan."

"I see," says the Moabite, "If only I had been born an Israelite, of one of the tribes of Israel." He looks more closely, and sees one of the priests, having offered a sacrifice at the brazen altar and cleansed himself at the brazen laver go into the tabernacle interior. His eyes widen and he asks, "What's in there, inside that main building?"

"Oh," says the gatekeeper, "That's the tabernacle itself, inside there is a room containing a lampstand, a table and an altar of gold. The man you saw is a priest. He will tend the lamp, eat of the bread upon the table, and burn incense to the living God upon the golden altar."

"Ah," the Moabite sighs deeply, "I wish I were an Israelite so that I could do that. I should love to worship God in that holy place and help to trim the lamp, to offer Him incense, and to eat at that table."

"Oh no," says the man at the gate, "even I could not do that. To worship in the holy place one must not only be born an Israelite, one must be born of the tribe of Levi, and of the family of Aaron."

Sighing again he says, "I wish, I wish I had been born of Israel of the tribe of Levi of the family of Aaron." Gazing longingly at the closed tabernacle door he says, "What else is in there?"

The gatekeeper continues, "There is a veil. It is a beautiful veil, I'm told, which divides the tabernacle in two. Beyond the veil is what we call the most holy place, 'The Holies of Holies.'"

"Yes, what's in the Holy of Holies?" The Moabite asks more interested than ever.

"There is a sacred chest in there called the Ark of the Covenant," answers the gatekeeper. "It contains the holy memorials of our past. It is made of gold, and we call that the mercy seat because God's presence rests there between the golden cherubim. See that pillar of cloud hovering over the tabernacle? Inside that is the Shekinah Glory the very presence of God; it comes to rest at the mercy seat."

Again a look of longing shadows the face of the man, "Oh," he says, "if only I were an Israelite of the tribe of Levi of the family of Aaron, a priest of God. I should go into the presence of God and worship. I would treasure His presence. I would go in every day and spend hours gazing upon God and daily worship Him there in His presence in the beauty of His holiness."

The gatekeeper busts in, "No, impossible, never, you couldn't do that even if you were a priest. Only the High priest of all Israel may go in there only He may go in, and only on the one day a year, and that only after much elaborate preparation. Actually he only goes in for a short time. He can never stop his work or sit down and then he must leave."

The Moabites heart yearns once more. "Oh," He cries,
sadly he turns away. He has no hope in all the world of ever
entering there.

The gatekeeper, himself, pondered all he thought to be privilege
as the chosen people, all he had taken for granted, and yet how far it
still left Him from the God he claimed as his own. In the last analysis
the tabernacle with all its symbolic construction spoke of exclusion.
Men were not allowed to enter into the place where the Shekinah
Glory of God shone.

You Dear Believer, are able to enter into that presence of God at
any and every moment and dwell there continuously. You are there
now, seated with Christ in the heavenlies at his right hand in Christ.
Picture that scene in your mind's eye. Be with Him there.

> Heb. 10: 19-22 "Therefore, brethren, since we have confidence to enter the holy place by the blood of Jesus, by a new and living way which He inaugurated for us through the veil, that is, His flesh, and since we have a great priest over the house of God, <u>let us draw near with a sincere heart in full assurance of faith,</u> having our hearts sprinkled clean from an evil conscience and our bodies washed with pure water."

I so long for you to understand your throne room privileges.

You are seated at the Right hand of the Father, the One of Power
from on High.

It is much truer that you are seated at the right hand of God than
that you are seated where you are now physically. God has *declared*
that you are seated in the heavenlies.

> Eph. 1:20 "which He brought about in Christ, when He raised Him from the dead and seated Him at His right hand in the heavenly places."

> Col. 4:1-4 "Therefore if you have been *raised up with Christ*, keep seeking the things above, where Christ is, seated *at the right hand* of God. Set your mind on the things above, not on the things that are on earth. For you have died and *your* life

is hidden with Christ in God. *When Christ,* who is our life, is revealed, then you also will be revealed with Him in glory."

Being at the right hand of God positionally means that you have the authority of a believer. Authority you ask? It is authority over the enemy, over resources and over those mountains that stand in the way of accomplishing the call of God. What might you do exercising this authority? You could intercede for members of the family of God, marshal the attack against evil forces, spiritually bomb the enemy, bring to bear angelic forces, draw on your position in Christ, bind demons, frustrate their turf, claim your spiritual rights, enlist the Spirit of God, call on your resources as an heir, request God's intervention, strengthen a fellow believer and rest in the Lord's attributes.

I have also found the need to focus on this truth in a number of evangelistic occasions. I have shared the gospel numerous times with different individuals who I would say have embraced New Age beliefs. That person's mind and thinking was so darkened that drawing on the authority of a believer and claiming appropriate truths was necessary. You can do this through a prayer most of the time. On rare occasions this may need to be spoken out loud. A number of times my conversations have been with those who held seriously false beliefs that went against the truth of the gospel. This next verse is applicable and can be claimed in a believer's authority.

2 cor. 4:3-6 "And even if our gospel is veiled, it is veiled to those who are perishing, in whose case the god of this world has blinded the minds of the unbelieving so that they might not see the light of the gospel of the glory of Christ, who is the image of God. For we do not preach ourselves but Christ Jesus as Lord, and ourselves as your bond-servants for Jesus' sake. For God, who said, "Light shall shine out of darkness," is the One who has shone in our hearts to give the Light of the knowledge of the glory of God in the face of Christ."

We cannot argue someone like this into heaven. The Holy Spirit needs to lift the veil. I guess what I am saying here is let's not just go about these situations as if they are just everyday situations, but engage in the real spiritual battle taking place and exercise our position with the authority of a believer.

These throne room truths are needed as we see greater and greater success in the progress of the gospel. I want to remind you the more success we see the closer we get to the heart of the enemy. The closer we get the more resistance we will encounter and the greater strongholds we will need to confront. You and I have the authority to command the enemy to be silent as we confront his lies with truth. We are able to bring people into a place where they experience Jesus who touches them and heals their wounds.

2 Cor. 10:3-5 "For though we walk in the flesh, we do not war according to the flesh, for the weapons of our warfare are not of the flesh, but divinely powerful for the destruction of fortresses. We are destroying speculations and every lofty thing raised up against the knowledge of God, and we are taking every thought captive to the obedience of Christ,"

40) Reign with Christ

2 tim.2:12a "If we endure, we will also reign with Him;

We are going to reign with Jesus who is king of the universe. He is the bridegroom and we as the church are His bride. He is the king and the church is His queen.

There is a scene in "Star Wars, The Empire Strikes Back" that captures the sense of what I want us to realize. Luke Skywalker and Darth Vader are in the heat of a light saber battle. Luke has already suffered the loss of a hand. He is hanging from scaffolding as Vader begins to unfold his relationship to Luke.

I saw the movies in the order of their release so as Darth shares in his breathy way, "Luke I am your father," you could feel the audience in the theater trying to will Luke to reject the idea. But Vader continues, "Luke come to the dark side and together we can defeat the emperor and together we can rule the Empire, Luke this is your destiny!" I got chills as I heard that the first time. Darth Vader was making Luke a sincere offer. It was one that was on the side of evil, but it was a grand offer of epic proportions.

Jesus has given you an offer, Believer, that exceeds that of the one offered Luke. Jesus has made you part of His royal Bride. He is coming in glory and will establish his eternal kingdom here on earth to reign as king of the entire created universe. Believers will rule with him in glory.

He will present us as His bride for the entire universe to see at the wedding feast of the lamb. The verses below highlight this truth.

Col. 3:1-4 "Therefore if you have been raised up with Christ, keep seeking the things above, where Christ is, seated at the right hand of God. Set your mind on the things above, not on the things that are on earth. For you have died and your life is hidden with Christ in God. When Christ, who is our life, is revealed, then you also will be revealed with Him in glory."

This is your destiny! We are the church triumphant. Since we will one day reign throughout the universe with our Savior and Lord there is no way we should act like losers now. The weight of this reality hit me as I was reading C.S. Lewis' book "Out of the Silent Planet".

The main character Ransom in Lewis' story, is kidnapped by two men and taken to Mars in a spaceship. These two men, he discovers, have evil intentions for the abundant gold found on the fourth planet from the sun. There are angelic beings who are the rulers on all other planets. Ransom discovers through the angelic beings the very nature of the universe. The ruler on Earth has become bent because he has chosen evil. Throughout the universe Earth is known as the silent planet, the only silent planet. Because of evil, it is out of communication with all the rest of creation.

The creatures and angels are not able to know what has occurred on Earth. Maledil, who is the second person of the trinity and ruler of the universe, has left heaven and gone to the silent planet. The angelic beings are amazed at Maledil's reason for going and are further baffled that He is now in the appearance of a human, forever to remain as the God man.

133

Now here is what clicked for me. The God of the universe has taken to Himself, human form. Okay I think I get that, Lord. That means that You, God the Son are not a Martian. You are not a Vulcan or ET or someone who looks like Yoda. You are not a transformer, but You have now forever taken the form of man, eternally identified with us. You are seated at this very moment on the throne of God and You are an earthman. Dearest Jesus, God in the flesh, that is radical! Lord, of all the planets in the universe you came to ours. God the Son, King of the universe is an earthman. Dear believer, you will reign with Him. That is your destiny.

> Phil.2:6-11 "who, although He existed in the form of God, did not regard equality with God a thing to be grasped, but emptied Himself, taking the form of a bond-servant, and being made in the likeness of men. Being found in appearance as a man, He humbled Himself by becoming obedient to the point of death, even death on a cross. For this reason also, God highly exalted Him, and bestowed on Him the name which is above every name, so that at the name of Jesus EVERY KNEE WILL BOW, of those who are in heaven and on earth and under the earth, and that every tongue will confess that Jesus Christ is Lord, to the glory of God the Father."

Every tongue will confess, That Jesus (an earthman) Christ (the Messiah) is Lord (Yahweh, LORD God). My Friend, do you see how this elevates your place in the universe? Is this stretching your understanding of who you are and the significance of your future? Royal blood flows through your veins. You are called to win the world for the King, can you see why you can believe God for this?

Brothers and Sisters this is who we are! We as the Christian community are surrounded by a mountain of truth. So why is it we too often look like a bunch of tourists standing around gawking, merely taking in the view like sight seers instead of looking, thinking and acting like fellow-heirs.

Do you wonder what God's heart is? Look at Ephesians chapter one. Notice the words I have emphasized in italics.

Eph.1:3-21 "Blessed be the God and Father of our Lord Jesus Christ, who has blessed us with every spiritual blessing in the heavenly places in Christ, just as He chose us in Him before the foundation of the world, that we would be holy and blameless before Him. In love He predestined us to adoption as sons through Jesus Christ to Himself, according to the kind intention of His will, *to the praise of the glory of His grace,* which He freely bestowed on us in the Beloved. In Him we have redemption through His blood, the forgiveness of our trespasses, according to the riches of His grace which He lavished on us. In all wisdom and insight He made known to us the mystery of His will, according to His kind intention which He purposed in Him with a view to an administration suitable to the fullness of the times, that is, the summing up of all things in Christ, things in the heavens and things on the earth. In Him also we have obtained an inheritance, having been predestined according to His purpose who works all things after the counsel of His will, to the end that we who were the first to hope in Christ would be *to the praise of His glory.* In Him, you also, after listening to the message of truth, the gospel of your salvation -having also believed, you were sealed in Him with the Holy Spirit of promise, who is given as a pledge of our inheritance, with a view to the redemption of God's own possession, *to the praise of His glory.*

The Father has chosen us and blessed us. The Son has redeemed us and given us an inheritance. We have been sealed in the Holy Spirit of Promise. Why did He do this? He did this as three times stated to the Praise of His glory and of His grace, to the praise of His glory and to the praise of His glory. It was not done for the enhancement of our self-images, nor was it done for the indulgence of our "name it, claim it" appetites. The Lord did it for the sake of His glory. So for God's sake we are expected to live in our position in Christ. Imagine with me His heart.

"Hello My Children. Are any of you listening to these truths? Are you hearing them with your heart and mind? Are you interested?"

"Hey Lord, You're great! All this positional truth stuff sure is amazing. Really, it is too amazing; I would feel I am being too bold to ask."

"Too bold?! You're my child, run into my arms. Dear One, this is not simply for you, it is my call to you for the praise of My glory."

"Where are you Lord?"

"I'm in the throne room."

"Wow, I'll bet that's something awesome. I would love to see it."

"Well sure, you are my child. You are royalty and as a son/daughter of the King of the universe. you are in here too.

1. "No I'm working too hard. You know, I'm trying to be obedient. I'm trying to get there."
    "Trying? Jesus was obedient, you're in Him. You are a son not a slave."
2. "You know I need to be a little more spiritual."
    "You are alive, born anew. You are indwelt by the Holy Spirit."
3. "I'm so young. When I get older, maybe then I can get to the throne room."
    "Ever read Eph. 2:6? You are seated in Christ in the heavenly places."
4. "Don't I need an experience? I lack some spiritual high don't I?"
    "You have Christ! (Col.210) you are complete in Him!"
5. "I'm trying to please You Lord!"
    "I am thoroughly pleased with Jesus. You are in Jesus I am thoroughly pleased with you."
6. "Can't be, no I'm not good enough."
    "Yes, but Jesus is! Like I said, you're in Jesus!"
7. "Well, I am improving, maybe when I get a better self-image, and then I'll believe this stuff. You know, I'm reading 'Search for Significance.'"
    "Your life is hidden in Christ."
8. "Lord if you really knew me you wouldn't say that."
    "I know you more intimately than you know yourself!"
9. "It's so hard. I'm just getting by. My family does not understand. I'm worn out. I just don't have the necessary means."

"Come unto ME all ye who are weary with heavy burdens. I will give you true rest. Take My yoke. I am your Father, you are My heir. I have that trust fund set up. You trust. I fund."

10. "I need to go to seminary and learn all about this."
"Read your Bible."
11. "I need to learn Greek."
"I speak English!!"
12. "How do I get there? I want to be there! What do I need?
"You only need to open your eyes you're already here!"

Eph. 1:18,19 " I pray that the *eyes of your heart may be enlightened*, so that you will know what is the hope of His calling, what are the riches of the glory of His inheritance in the saints, and what is the surpassing greatness of His power toward us who believe. These are in accordance with the working of the strength of His might which He brought about in Christ, when He raised Him from the dead and seated Him at His right hand in the heavenly places, far above all rule and authority and power and dominion, and every name that is named, not only in this age but also in the one to come."

God is calling us to believe His Word. Paul prays that we come to 1) A clearer understanding of the greatness of our Lord, 2) the vastness of our inheritance, 3) the endlessness of our precious hope and 4) the limitlessness of His power toward us. His prayer is earnest that our minds, our insights, that the eyes of our hearts would truly see these things. That is his supreme desire that we will fully realize what our identity in Christ means.

Are not our hearts stirred when Mel Gibson and Russell Crowe play these heroic characters in the "Patriot"," Braveheart" and "Gladiator". We have a never ending amount of resources to take on Biblical heroics because we are THE CHURCH TRIUMPHANT.

So then Beloved if it is for God's glory, if it is for His sake, let us live out Eph.1:23 "The fullness of Him who fills everything in every way (NIV)." God has done all this for His glory. So for God's sake Believer, live in your position!!Yes, *for God's sake* live in it!

CPSIA information can be obtained at www.ICGtesting.com
Printed in the USA
BVOW08s1918190214

345435BV00001B/3/P